T[illegible] Subject Was Roses

A PLAY
IN TWO ACTS

By Frank D. Gilroy

Winner of the 1965
Pulitzer Prize
for Drama.

SAMUEL FRENCH, INC.

45 West 25th Street — NEW YORK 10010
7623 Sunset Boulevard — HOLLYWOOD 90046
LONDON — *TORONTO*

ISBN 0 573 61592 6

Printed in U.S.A.

THE SUBJECT WAS ROSES, by Frank D. Gilroy, directed by Ulu Grosbard, setting by Edgar Lansbury, lighting by Jules Fisher, costumes by Donald Foote, was presented by Edgar Lansbury on May 25, 1964, at the Royale Theatre, N.Y.C.

CAST

(*In Order of Appearance*)

JOHN CLEARY .... *Jack Albertson*

NETTIE CLEARY .... *Irene Dailey*

TIMMY CLEARY .... *Martin Sheen*

Production Stage Manager, Paul Leaf

SCENES

The action takes place in a middle-class apartment, in May, 1946.

ACT ONE

SCENE 1: Saturday morning.

SCENE 2: Saturday afternoon.

SCENE 3: Two A.M. Sunday morning.

ACT TWO

SCENE 1: Sunday morning.

SCENE 2: Sunday evening.

SCENE 3: Two A.M. Monday morning.

SCENE 4: Monday morning.

The Subject Was Roses

ACT ONE

SCENE 1

PLACE: *The kitchen and living room of a middle-class apartment in the West Bronx. A doorway Upstage links the two rooms. An invisible wall divides them. The living room is furnished with the heavy upholstered pieces (replete with antimacassars) considered fashionable in the late twenties and early thirties. There is evidence of a party given the night before: a beer keg; a stack of camp chairs; a sagging banner, hand lettered—"Welcome Home Timmy."*

TIME: *A Saturday morning in May of 1946.*

AT RISE: *The Stage is empty. After a moment, a man of fifty,* JOHN CLEARY, *enters from* U. L. *bedroom and stands contemplating the living room. Then he crosses* R. *to kitchen and looks at an army jacket hanging on the broom closet door. The army jacket bears an infantry division patch; corporal chevrons; service ribbons, including the ETO with two battle stars, and a presidential unit citation; four "Hershey Bars," marking two years of overseas duty; and the "Ruptured Duck," signifying recent discharge.* JOHN CLEARY'S *expression as he regards the jacket is one of almost reverent curiosity. He touches the jacket; feels the material; traces the outline of the chevrons inquiringly. Now, on an impulse, he takes the jacket from the hanger; dons it furtively; is enjoying what is obviously a secret moment when he hears a KEY turn in the front door. Quickly returning the jacket to the hanger, he takes a seat at* L. *side of the kitchen table and appears engrossed in a newspaper when the door opens and his wife,* NETTIE, *forty-five, enters with a bundle of groceries. She crosses to kitchen counter and draws window curtains. She takes syrup and cream from grocery bag; then pours orange juice into a glass.*

NETTIE. It's a lovely day. . . . Timmy still asleep?

JOHN. Haven't heard him. . . . Better give me mine.

NETTIE. I thought we'd all have breakfast together.

JOHN. I have to go downtown.

NETTIE. (*Putting things in refrigerator.*) Today?

JOHN. Ruskin wants to see me. (*She regards him a moment, then begins to set the food before him.*) I'm going to stop at Saint Francis on the way . . . to offer a prayer of thanks.

NETTIE. (*Serving him the juice.*) Toast?

JOHN. Yes. . . . All those casualties and he never got a scratch. We're very lucky.

NETTIE. (*Puts bread in toaster, then pours coffee.*) What do you want on it?

JOHN. Marmalade. . . . The Freeman boy dead. The Mullin boy crippled for life. . . . Makes you wonder. . . . Think he enjoyed the party?

NETTIE. (*Crossing to table with coffee.*) He seemed to.

JOHN. First time I ever saw him take a drink.

NETTIE. He drank too much.

JOHN. You don't get out of the army every day.

NETTIE. He was sick during the night.

JOHN. Probably the excitement.

NETTIE. It was the whiskey. You should have stopped him.

JOHN. For three years he's gotten along fine without anyone telling him what to do.

NETTIE. I had to hold his head.

JOHN. No one held his head in the army.

NETTIE. (*Serves him marmalade, then crosses back to counter.*) That's what *he* said.

JOHN. But that didn't stop *you*.

NETTIE. He's not in the army any more.

JOHN. It was a boy that walked out of this house three years ago. It's a man that's come back in.

NETTIE. You sound like a recruiting poster.

JOHN. *You* sound ready to repeat the old mistakes.

NETTIE. (*Turns to him.*) Mistakes?

JOHN. Pardon me.

NETTIE. You said mistakes.

JOHN. Slip of the tongue.

NETTIE. I'd like to know what mistakes you're referring to.

JOHN. The coffee's excellent.

NETTIE. I'd really like to know.

JOHN. He was eighteen when he went away. Until that time, he showed no special skill at anything, but you treated him like he was a protege.

NETTIE. (*Brings toast to table.*) I think you mean prodigy.

JOHN. What I really mean is baby.

NETTIE. For a baby he certainly did well in the army.

JOHN. (*Spreading marmalade on toast.*) I didn't say he *was* a baby. I said you treated him like one.

NETTIE. You were surprised he did well. You didn't think he'd last a week. (*She takes off her sweater and puts it on kitchen chair.*)

JOHN. Bless us and save us said Mrs. O'Davis.

NETTIE. Do you know why you were surprised?

JOHN. Joy, joy said Mrs. Malloy.

NETTIE. Because you never understood him.

JOHN. Mercy, mercy, said old Mrs. Percy.

NETTIE. (*Crosses to counter for apron and puts it on.*) I never doubted that he'd do as well as anyone else.

JOHN. Where he's concerned, you never doubted period. If he came in here right now and said he could fly, you'd help him out the window.

NETTIE. (*Crosses to* R. *chair.*) If you're saying I have confidence in him you're right. And why not? Who knows him better?

JOHN. Is there more coffee?

NETTIE. He's exceptional.

JOHN. Here we go again.

NETTIE. Yes—exceptional!

JOHN. In what way?

NETTIE. (*Crosses to stove, gets coffee pot, brings it back to table and pours.*) I refuse to discuss it.

JOHN. A person who's going to be famous usually drops a *few* clues by the time they're twenty-one.

NETTIE. I didn't say famous—I said exceptional.

JOHN. What's the difference?

NETTIE. You wouldn't understand.

JOHN. Here's something you better understand—You can't treat him as though he'd never been away. He's not a kid.

NETTIE. (*Crossing back to stove with coffee pot.*) If you had stopped him from drinking too much that would have been treating him like a kid?

JOHN. This is where I came in.

NETTIE. He was trying to keep up with you and you knew it.

JOHN. You sound like you're jealous.

NETTIE. The two of you so busy drinking you hardly paid attention to anyone else. (*Hangs shopping bag on counter door knob, puts purse in drawer.*)

JOHN. You *are* jealous!

NETTIE. Don't be absurd.

JOHN. He and I got along better yesterday than we ever did before and you're jealous. (*She turns away.*) Well, well, well. (*He finishes the last of his coffee. Rises to leave.*)

NETTIE. Can't Ruskin wait till Monday?

JOHN. (*Crosses to counter and gets toothpick from drawer.*) No. And don't pretend you're disappointed. What a charming little breakfast you and he will have together.

NETTIE. (*Picks up his napkin and folds it.*) You're welcome to stay.

JOHN. My ears are burning a ady.

NETTIE. I've never said a word against you and you know it.

JOHN. Don't forget my excursion to Montreal.

NETTIE. It was always your own actions that turned him against you.

JOHN. And the convention— Don't leave that out. (*He goes toward living room.*)

NETTIE. The curtains. (*He regards her. She crosses in toward him.*) The curtains for Timmy's room. They're coming today.

JOHN. I don't know anything about curtains.

NETTIE. Yes, you do.

JOHN. I do not.

NETTIE. They'll be ten dollars.

JOHN. What's the matter with the old ones?

(TIMMY CLEARY, *twenty-one, wearing army sun-tans, open at the neck, emerges from his room,* D. L., *starts toward the kitchen, is arrested by their voices; stops, listens.*)

NETTIE. They're worn out.

JOHN. They look all right to me.

NETTIE. They aren't all right.

JOHN. Ten dollars for curtains.

NETTIE. Timmy will want to bring friends home.

JOHN. (*Crosses* D. R.) The old squeeze play.

(TIMMY *puts his hands over his ears.*)

NETTIE. (*Crosses to below table.*) Are you going to give me the money?

JOHN. (*He extracts a bill from his wallet, slaps it on the kitchen table.*) Here! (*Starts* U. R. *of table as if to go.*)

NETTIE. I need five dollars for the house.

JOHN. (*Crosses* D.) I gave you fifteen yesterday.

NETTIE. That went for the party.

JOHN. That party cost close to a hundred dollars.

NETTIE. It was worth it.

JOHN. Did I say it wasn't? (*He takes another bill from his wallet, first turning away so that* NETTIE *can't see how much is in wallet, and puts it down.*) There.

(TIMMY *goes back, slams the door of his room to alert them, then approaches the kitchen.* NETTIE *and* JOHN *compose themselves cheerfully as* TIMMY, *equally cheerful, enters.* JOHN *crosses to* TIMMY. NETTIE *stays* D. R.)

TIMMY. Good morning. (*Shakes hands with* JOHN.)

JOHN. Champ.

NETTIE. 'Morning, son. (*He crosses and kisses her on cheek.*)

JOHN. We thought you were going to sleep all day. (*Sits* L. *chair.*)

TIMMY. I smelled the coffee. (*Sits* C. *chair.*)

JOHN. Mother said you were sick during the night.

TIMMY. I'm fine now.

JOHN. I was a little rocky myself.

TIMMY. I wonder why.

(*They BOTH laugh.*)

NETTIE. (*To* JOHN.) What time is your appointment?

JOHN. Eleven-fifteen.

NETTIE. It's twenty-five of.

JOHN. (*Rises, crosses* L. *to* TIMMY.) Mr. Ruskin wants to see me.

TIMMY. That's too bad.

(NETTIE *pours juice at counter.*)

JOHN. Why?

TIMMY. Thought we might take in the Giant game.

NETTIE. (*To* JOHN.) Why don't you? (*Crosses to* TIMMY *with juice.*)

JOHN. You know I can't. (*To* TIMMY.) This thing with Ruskin means a sure sale.

TIMMY. I understand.

JOHN. We'll go tomorrow.

NETTIE. (*Crossing to counter to get out waffle iron.*) My mother expects us for dinner tomorrow.

JOHN. (*He looks at* NETTIE *as though he might say something; thinks better of it; turns to* TIMMY.) How about *next* Saturday?

TIMMY. All right.

JOHN. We'll get box seats—the works.

TIMMY. Sounds fine.

JOHN. Swell. (*Gets his jacket and hat from living room closet.*)

NETTIE. (TIMMY *up, pushes* JOHN'S *chair under table.*) What time will you be home?

JOHN. I'll call you.

NETTIE. I'll be at my mother's.

JOHN. (*Appraising* TIMMY, *who has risen.*) I understand none of your old clothes fit.

TIMMY. That's right.

JOHN. Meet me downtown on Monday and we'll get you some new ones.

TIMMY. Okay.

(JOHN *feints a jab.* TIMMY *covers up. They spar good-naturedly until* TIMMY *drops his hands.*)

JOHN. I still think I can take you.

TIMMY. I wouldn't be surprised.

JOHN. See you later.

TIMMY. Right.

JOHN. (*He moves toward the door, stops before the army jacket; indicates one of the ribbons.*) What did you say this one was for?

TIMMY. It's a combat infantry badge.

JOHN. How about that?

TIMMY. (*Crosses Upstage.* NETTIE *is busy at sink.*) It's not as important as it sounds.

JOHN. We'll have to sit down and have a real talk. I want to hear all about it.

TIMMY. All right.

JOHN. It's great to have you home.

TIMMY. It's great to be home.

JOHN. The Mullin boy crippled. The Freeman boy dead. We're very lucky.

TIMMY. I know.

JOHN. I'm stopping off at Saint Francis this morning to offer a prayer of thanks. . . . See you later.

TIMMY. Right. (*Crosses to kitchen door.*)

(JOHN *exits from the apartment.* TIMMY *looks after him.*)

NETTIE. (*At counter.*) How did you sleep?

TIMMY. (*Crosses* R.) Fine. . . . How's he feeling?

NETTIE. All right.

TIMMY. He looks a lot older.

NETTIE. It's been two years. . . . It must have seemed strange. (*He glances at her.*) Sleeping in your own bed.

TIMMY. (*Turning away again.*) Yes. . . . How's his business?

NETTIE. Who knows?

TIMMY. The coffee market's off.

NETTIE. I hope you're hungry.

TIMMY. I can't get over the change in him.

NETTIE. Guess what we're having for breakfast.

TIMMY. It's not just the way he looks.

NETTIE. *Guess what we're having for breakfast.* (*He turns to her.*) Guess what we're having.

TIMMY. What?

NETTIE. Guess.

TIMMY. I don't know.

NETTIE. Yes, you do.

TIMMY. No.

NETTIE. Sure you do.

TIMMY. What is it?

NETTIE. You're fooling.

TIMMY. What is it?

NETTIE. What's your favorite?

TIMMY. Bacon and eggs?

NETTIE. Now I know you're fooling.

TIMMY. No.

NETTIE. I forgot what a tease you were.

TIMMY. I'm not teasing.

NETTIE. (*Shows syrup.*) Waffles. We're having waffles.

TIMMY. Fine. (*Sits.*)

NETTIE. You used to be crazy about waffles.

TIMMY. I still am.

NETTIE. (*Crosses* U. L. *of him.*) I've got the waffle batter ready.

TIMMY. Swell.

NETTIE. Your first morning home, you're entitled to whatever you want.

TIMMY. I want waffles.

NETTIE. (*Crosses* D. L. *of him.*) I used the last egg in the batter.

TIMMY. *I want waffles.*

NETTIE. Really?

TIMMY. (*Raises his hand.*) Cross my heart.

NETTIE. All right.

(*She gets batter from refrigerator, brings it down to show him. He looks at it, takes his juice glass, drinks, then puts glass in sink and crosses to window. She mixes batter at table.*)

TIMMY. I see a new butcher.

NETTIE. Quite a few new stores.

TIMMY. Pop said the Bremens moved.

NETTIE. And the Costellos. . . . Remember old Zimmer the tailor?

TIMMY. Sure.

NETTIE. A few weeks ago a woman brought him a coat she wanted altered. Zimmer started to fix it, then very politely excused himself, went up to the roof and jumped. No one knows why.

TIMMY. Who was the woman?

NETTIE. Mrs. Levin.

TIMMY. That explains it.

NETTIE. That's not funny.

TIMMY. (*Turns to her.*) Sorry.

NETTIE. What a thing to say.

TIMMY. I said I'm sorry.

NETTIE. (*Crosses above table.*) I'm surprised at you.

TIMMY. (*Two steps in to her.*) Bless us and save us.

NETTIE. *What?*

TIMMY. Bless us and save us. As in "Bless us and save us said Mrs. O'Davis; Joy, joy said Mrs. Malloy. . . ." (*She regards him incredulously.*) What's the matter?

NETTIE. I never expected to hear that nonsense from *you.*

TIMMY. It beats swearing.

NETTIE. You used to cover your ears when your father said it.

TIMMY. (*Salutes with mock solemnity.*) I'll never say it again.

NETTIE. *Don't talk to me like that!* . . . I'm sorry. I don't know what's wrong with me this morning. I don't think I slept well. . . . Too much excitement—the party and all. (*She resumes the preparation of breakfast: Pours batter on the waffle iron while he, still not recovered from her outburst, studies her.*) Will you have bacon with it?

TIMMY. (*Sits* L. *chair at table.*) Just the waffles will be fine.

NETTIE. Did you like the party?

TIMMY. Yes.

NETTIE. I wish the house had looked better. (*Puts her sweater and his army jacket in closet.*)

TIMMY. What's wrong with it?

NETTIE. It needs painting. The sofa's on its last legs. And the rugs . . . (*Crosses to counter.*) Well now that you're here I'll get it all fixed up.

TIMMY. It looks fine to me.

NETTIE. (*Crosses* L.) I still can't believe you're here.

TIMMY. I find it a little hard to believe myself.

NETTIE. You *are* here?

TIMMY. Want to pinch me? . . . go ahead. (*She hesi-*

tates. He holds out his hand.) Go on. (*She takes his hand.*) Believe it now? (*She continues to hold his hand. He becomes uneasy.*) Hey. (*Oblivious to his resistance, she still clings to his hand.*) What are you doing? (*She persists. His agitation mounts.*) Cut it out . . . *Cut it out!* (*He jerks free of her and jumps up; immediately tries to make light of it.*) One pinch to a customer. . . . House rule. (*She regards him mutely.*) The waffles must be ready; the light on the iron went out. (*She just looks at him.*) Isn't that what it means when that little light goes out? (*She looks at him a moment more, then goes to the waffle iron, lifts the cover; starts to remove the waffles; stops; moves to a chair; sits; folds her hands in her lap and begins to cry.*) What's the matter? . . . What's wrong? . . . What is it? . . . *What is it?*

NETTIE. (*Continuing to cry.*) They stuck.

TIMMY. What? (*Crosses and looks at waffles.*)

NETTIE. Why did they have to stick today?

TIMMY. The waffles?

NETTIE. I can't remember the last time they stuck.

TIMMY. What's that to cry about?

NETTIE. I've looked forward to this morning for three years and nothing's right.

TIMMY. Why do you say that?

NETTIE. Not one thing.

TIMMY. What isn't right?

NETTIE. Not one single thing.

TIMMY. (*Crosses* L. *of table.*) Will you please stop?

NETTIE. The things you've been saying— Your attitude.

TIMMY. What things? What attitude?

NETTIE. You haven't even asked about Willis.

TIMMY. . . . How is he?

NETTIE. Every time I look at you, you avoid me.

TIMMY. (*Turning away.*) That's ridiculous.

NETTIE. You're doing it now.

TIMMY. I am not!

NETTIE. How could you forget waffles were your favorite?

TIMMY. I just forgot.

NETTIE. Then you must have forgotten a lot of things.

TIMMY. *I'll tell you one thing I didn't forget.* (*She looks at him.*) The dance. (*No reaction from her.*) The one we were going to have the first morning I was home.

NETTIE. What made you think of that?

TIMMY. It's been on my mind all along.

NETTIE. I'll bet.

TIMMY. I was about to turn the radio on when you started crying.

NETTIE. I'll bet.

TIMMY. If you're through, I'll do it now. (*Crosses to doorway and turns.*) Are you through?

NETTIE. I haven't danced in so long I've probably forgotten how.

TIMMY. (*He goes to the living room, snaps on the RADIO; dials to a band playing a slow fox trot; returns to the kitchen.*) Shall we have a go at it?

NETTIE. I can't remember the last time I danced.

TIMMY. (*Crosses* L. *of table.*) Come on.

NETTIE. You really want to?

TIMMY. Yes.

NETTIE. (*Rising and crossing to him.*) You asked for it.

TIMMY. That a girl. (*He puts his arms about her.*) Here we go. (*They move smoothly, gracefully.*) Forgot how to dance—who you kidding?

NETTIE. I guess it's one of those things you never forget.

TIMMY. Remember this? (*He goes into a maneuver that she follows perfectly; she pirouettes.*) You've been taking lessons.

NETTIE. Of course.

(*They dance from the kitchen into the living room.*)

TIMMY. Come here off-ten?

NETTIE. Foist time.

TIMMY. Me likewise. . . . By yuhself?

NETTIE. Widda goil friend.

(*SONG ends.*)

ANNOUNCER'S VOICE. That's all the time we have on Dance Parade this morning. I hope—

TIMMY. Don't move! (*He goes to the radio; dials; picks up a POLKA BAND going full blast.*) What do you say?

NETTIE. The spirit's willing.

TIMMY. Let's go! (*He moves furniture back and they take off.*) Not bad. . . . Not bad.

NETTIE. What will the neighbors think?

TIMMY. The worst. (*The rhythm begins to accelerate.*) We're coming into the home stretch. Hang on. (*They move faster and faster.*)

NETTIE. I'm getting dizzy.

(*As they whirl about the room they begin to laugh.*)

TIMMY. Hang on.

NETTIE. I can't do any more. (*The laughter grows.*)

TIMMY. Hang on!

NETTIE. I can't! (*The laughter becomes hysterical.*)

TIMMY. Hang on! Hang on!

NETTIE. I can't! I . . .

(*They trip; collapse to the floor, below couch.*)

TIMMY. You all right?

NETTIE. I think so.

(*Both breathe laboredly. The laughter subsides. He snaps the RADIO off, then sits on the floor facing her, leaning against chair* L.)

TIMMY. I'm dead. . . . Absolutely dead.

NETTIE. So am I.

TIMMY. I can't remember the last time I laughed like that.

NETTIE. I can. . . . We were driving to the lake and stopped at that dinky carnival.

TIMMY. The time I got you to go on that ride.

NETTIE. Your father thought we'd lost our minds. He kept begging the man to stop the engine.

TIMMY. Which made us laugh all the harder.

NETTIE. Know something?

TIMMY. What?

NETTIE. I really believe you're here now.

TIMMY. So do I.

NETTIE. What are you going to do today?

TIMMY. I don't know.

NETTIE. Why don't you come to Mama's with me?

TIMMY. We're going there for dinner tomorrow.

NETTIE. Willis would love to see you.

TIMMY. I'll see him tomorrow.

NETTIE. When we told him you were coming home he began to sing. It's the first time he's done that in months.

TIMMY. All right, I'll go.

NETTIE. We won't stay long.

TIMMY. All right.

(*The door opens and* JOHN *enters; takes off his hat; sees them on the floor.*)

JOHN. Well, hello. (*Crosses* D. R. TIMMY *rises.*) Don't get up on my account.

TIMMY. We were dancing and fell down.

NETTIE. (*To* JOHN.) What did you forget?

(TIMMY *replaces furniture.*)

JOHN. Nothing.

NETTIE. (*Rising.*) Why did you come back?

JOHN. I changed my mind. (*Crosses* R. *to* TIMMY.) If you still want to go to the ball game, it's a date.

NETTIE. What about Ruskin?

JOHN. The hell with him. (*To* TIMMY.) Still want to go?

TIMMY. Yes.

NETTIE. What about Willis?

JOHN. (*Turns to her.*) What *about* Willis?

NETTIE. Timmy was going to see him this afternoon.

TIMMY. I'll see him tomorrow.

NETTIE. I told him you'd be over today.

TIMMY. Before you even asked me?

NETTIE. I thought sure you'd want to.

TIMMY. You had no right to do that.

NETTIE. What will I tell him?

TIMMY. Tell him I'll be there tomorrow.

NETTIE. He'll be disappointed.

TIMMY. That's not my fault.

JOHN. The game starts at twelve.

TIMMY. Just have to get my tie. (*Crosses toward his bedroom.*)

NETTIE. You haven't eaten.

TIMMY. We'll grab something on the way. (*He exits.*)

JOHN. I came out of Saint Francis and started for the subway. Was half-way there when I thought of Mr. Freeman: What wouldn't *he* give to be able to spend a day with his son? . . . It made me turn around and come back. (*She just looks at him.*) You're mad. (*No reply.*) You told me to take him to the game.

NETTIE. And you always do what I tell you. (*Crosses to kitchen and starts clearing table.*)

JOHN. Bless us and save us. (*Crosses Upstage a few steps.*)

(TIMMY, *knotting his tie, reappears. Snaps to attention, salutes.*)

TIMMY. Corporal Cleary reporting for duty.

JOHN. Kiss your mother goodbye.

TIMMY. That's not a duty. (*He crosses to* NETTIE *at table and kisses her on cheek. She receives the kiss impassively, then goes to sink.*) So long, Mom. (*She doesn't answer.* TIMMY *gets his jacket from closet.*)

JOHN. We won't be late.

(*He and* TIMMY *exit. She gets apron from chair and puts it on, as:*)

CURTAIN

ACT ONE

SCENE 2

TIME: *Late afternoon—the same day.*

AT RISE: JOHN *and* TIMMY *enter the apartment.* TIMMY *carries a bouquet of red roses.* JOHN *has just concluded a joke and they are both laughing.*

JOHN. I haven't told that one in years.

TIMMY. I was considered a very funny fellow: Thanks to you.

JOHN. Hello? . . . Anybody home? (*No answer.*) Still at her mother's.

TIMMY. (*Indicating the roses.*) I better put these in water.

(*They move into the kitchen.* TIMMY *puts roses on counter, gets vase from under sink, fills it with water and arranges roses on Downstage end of counter.*)

JOHN. Stand another beer?

TIMMY. Sure.

(JOHN *gets two bottles of beer from the refrigerator.*)

JOHN. (*Opening the beers.*) How did you remember all those jokes of mine?

TIMMY. Just came to me. (*Takes off his jacket and throws it on chair.*)

JOHN. I don't remember most of them myself. . . . (*Hands* TIMMY *a beer.*) Here you go.

TIMMY. Thanks.
JOHN. What'll we drink to?
TIMMY. The Chicago Cubs.
JOHN. Think it'll help them?
TIMMY. Can it hurt?
JOHN. (*Raising the bottle.*) To the Cubs.
TIMMY. To the Cubs.

(*Both drink.*)

JOHN. Sixteen to three.
TIMMY. I'm still glad we went. (*Sits.*)
JOHN. So am I. (*Drinks.*) That was a beautiful catch Ott made.
TIMMY. Yes.
JOHN. For a moment I thought he lost it in the sun (TIMMY *says nothing.* JOHN *drinks.*) So they really went for the old man's jokes?
TIMMY. Especially the ones about Uncle Mike.
JOHN. Such as?
TIMMY. The Pennsylvania Hotel gag.
JOHN. Columbus told that one to the Indians.
TIMMY. Uncle Mike was a famous man in our outfit.
JOHN. Joking aside, he was quite a guy. Stood six-three. Weighed close to two-fifty.
TIMMY. I remember his picture.
JOHN. He was in the Spanish American War.
TIMMY. I know.
JOHN. Got hit by a bullet once that knocked him out. When he came to, he was lying in a field full of wounded men. The ones that were sure goners were marked with yellow tags so no one would waste time on them. The others had blue tags. Mike found a yellow tag around his wrist. The fellow next to him who was unconscious had a blue one. Quick as a wink Mike switched the tags and . . . How about that? I'm telling *you* war stories. Go on—you do the talking.
TIMMY. About what?
JOHN. You must have seen some pretty bad things.

TIMMY. Not as much as a lot of others.

JOHN. Maybe you'd rather not talk about it.

TIMMY. I don't mind.

JOHN. I'd like to hear what you have to say.

TIMMY. I don't know how to begin.

JOHN. Anything that comes to mind.

TIMMY. Want to hear the bravest thing I ever did?

JOHN. Yes.

TIMMY. The first night we were in combat I slept with my boots off.

JOHN. Go on.

TIMMY. That's it.

JOHN. You slept with your boots off?

TIMMY. Doesn't sound like much, does it?

JOHN. Not off-hand.

TIMMY. The fellows who eventually cracked up were all guys who couldn't sleep. If I hadn't decided to take my boots off I'd have ended up being one of them.

JOHN. I see.

TIMMY. Want to know the smartest thing I did?

JOHN. Sure.

TIMMY. I never volunteered. One day the Lieutenant bawled me out for it. I said, "Sir, if there's anything you want me to do you tell me and I'll do it. But if you wait for me to volunteer you'll wait forever."

JOHN. What did he say to that?

TIMMY. Nothing printable. The fact is I wasn't a very good soldier, Pop.

JOHN. You did everything they asked you.

TIMMY. The good ones do more. You'd have been a good one.

JOHN. What makes you say that?

TIMMY. I can tell.

JOHN. Well, thanks.

TIMMY. You're welcome.

JOHN. It's one of the big regrets of my life that I was never in the service.

TIMMY. I know.

JOHN. The day World War One was declared I went to

the recruiting office. When they learned I was the sole support of the family, they turned me down.

TIMMY. I know.

JOHN. A lot of people made cracks. Especially guys like Clayton and Harper who waited to be drafted and then wangled safe jobs at Governor's Island and the Navy Yard. . . . I fixed their wagons one night; sent the army flying one way and the navy the other. That was the last about slacking I heard from *them*. . . . Still it bothers me—missing out on the whole thing. . . . I keep wondering what difference it might have made in my life. . . . And then I wonder how I'd have made out. . . . I wouldn't have settled for a desk job. I'd have gotten to the Front.

TIMMY. I'm sure of that.

JOHN. But once there, how would I have done?

TIMMY. Fine.

JOHN. How do you know?

TIMMY. You're a born fighter.

JOHN. They say a lot of fellows who were terrors as civilians turned to jelly when they heard those bullets.

TIMMY. Not you.

JOHN. It doesn't seem so. But you can't be sure. . . . That's always bothered me. (*Drinks the last of his beer.*) How about another?

TIMMY. Fine.

JOHN. (*Rises to cross; stops and turns.*) Maybe we shouldn't.

TIMMY. Why?

JOHN. Your mother blames me for your getting sick last night; says I encouraged you to drink too much.

TIMMY. It wasn't what I drank. It was the excitement.

JOHN. That's what I told her.

TIMMY. *I'll* open two more.

JOHN. All right. (*While* TIMMY *gets the beers,* JOHN *sits, regards the roses.* TIMMY *comes back with the beers.*) Her father used to send her roses every birthday. . . . A dozen red ones. . . . Never missed. . . . Even at the end.

TIMMY. Tell her they were your idea.

JOHN. What?

TIMMY. Tell her the roses were your idea.

JOHN. Why?

TIMMY. She'll get a kick out of it. . . . All right?

JOHN. If you like.

TIMMY. (*Opens a beer and hands it to him.*) Here you go.

JOHN. Thanks.

TIMMY. You call it this time.

JOHN. (*Raising his bottle.*) To the two nicest fellows in the house.

TIMMY. I'll buy that. (*They drink.* TIMMY *regards the bottle.*) Funny how you acquire a taste for things. (*Sits.*)

JOHN. Yes.

TIMMY. When I was a kid I couldn't even stand the smell of beer.

JOHN. Believe it or not I was the same.

TIMMY. We seem to have gotten over it.

JOHN. Yes. . . . Can I say something to you?

TIMMY. Sure.

JOHN. You won't take it the wrong way?

TIMMY. No.

JOHN. I owe you an apology.

TIMMY. For what?

JOHN. You were always sick; always home from school with one thing or another. I never thought you'd last in the army.

TIMMY. Neither did I.

JOHN. Really?

TIMMY. Really.

JOHN. When Doctor Goldman heard they took you he said it was ridiculous. When they put you in the infantry he said it was inhuman.

TIMMY. And when I survived?

JOHN. He said it was a miracle. (*Both laugh.*) I don't think it was a miracle. I think we just underestimated you. . . . Especially me. . . . That's what I wanted to apologize for.

TIMMY. Remember that corny thing you used to recite— About how a boy thinks his father is the greatest guy in the world until he's fifteen. Then the doubts start. By the time he's eighteen he's convinced his father is the worst guy in the world. At twenty-five the doubts start again. At thirty it occurs to him that the old man wasn't so bad after all. At forty—

JOHN. —What about it?

TIMMY. There's some truth to it.

JOHN. I think you've had too much to drink.

TIMMY. I'm not saying you're a saint.

JOHN. That's a relief.

TIMMY. But taking into account where you started from, and the obstacles you had to overcome, what you've done is something to be proud of.

JOHN. Well, thank you.

TIMMY. How many guys that you grew up with even turned out legitimate?

JOHN. Not many.

TIMMY. And most of *them* are still scraping along where they started.

JOHN. That's true.

TIMMY. How many years of school did you have?

JOHN. I had to quit after the fourth grade.

TIMMY. I've met college graduates who don't know nearly as much as you about the things that really count.

JOHN. Must have been Yale men.

TIMMY. I'm serious.

JOHN. Speaking of college . . . if you get into one of those big ones and it's more than the G.I. bill pays for, I'll help you out.

TIMMY. Thanks.

JOHN. That's just between you and me.

TIMMY. Why?

JOHN. I don't want people getting wrong notions.

TIMMY. About what?

JOHN. That I'm loaded.

TIMMY. *Are* you loaded?

JOHN. Don't be ridiculous.

TIMMY. That doesn't answer my question.

JOHN. The question's ridiculous.

TIMMY. (*Rises and crosses to* L. *of* JOHN.) That's still no answer.

JOHN. No, I'm not loaded.

TIMMY. How much do you have?

JOHN. What?

TIMMY. How much money do you have?

JOHN. Is this your idea of a joke?

TIMMY. No.

JOHN. Then why are you doing it?

TIMMY. I don't want to take money from you if you can't afford it.

JOHN. I can afford it.

TIMMY. Some of the places I applied at are pretty expensive.

JOHN. I can afford it!

TIMMY. Then you must be loaded.

JOHN. *I am not loaded!*

TIMMY. We have a summer place, a car. Now you tell me you can afford any school in the country. You must be fairly loaded.

JOHN. (*Rising.*) *If I hear that word once more, I'm marching right out the door!*

TIMMY. (*He is unable to control his laughter any longer; crosses* U. R.) You haven't changed a bit. (JOHN *regards his uncertainly.*) You look as though I'd asked you to betray your country.

JOHN. (*Against his will, he smiles.*) You son of a gun!

TIMMY. I really had you going.

JOHN. Some joke. (*Sits.*)

TIMMY. (*Crosses to* R. *of* JOHN.) Oh, say, Pop.

JOHN. What?

TIMMY. How much *do* you have?

JOHN. *Enough's enough!* (TIMMY *laughs anew; crosses to counter.*) I think we better change the subject.

TIMMY. How did you meet Mother? (JOHN *regards him.*) You said change the subject.

JOHN. You know all about that.

TIMMY. Just that you picked her up on the subway.

JOHN. It wasn't like that at all.

TIMMY. Then I don't know all about it.

JOHN. "Picked her up" makes it sound cheap.

TIMMY. Sorry.

JOHN. The first time I spoke to her was on the subway, but there's more to it.

TIMMY. Tell me. (*Sits on counter.*)

JOHN. Why?

TIMMY. I might become a writer and want to do a story about it someday.

JOHN. A writer?

TIMMY. Maybe.

JOHN. Well that's the first I heard about that.

TIMMY. Me, too. Must be the beer. . . . What year was it you met her?

JOHN. Nineteen twenty-one. . . . A writer?

TIMMY. A writer. . . . Where were you working then?

JOHN. At Emerson's. . . .

TIMMY. And?

JOHN. One morning I saw her walk by. That afternoon she passed again. Same the next day. Turned out she worked around the corner. I . . . You sure you want to hear this?

TIMMY. Uh-huh.

JOHN. One evening I happened to be leaving at the same time she did. Turned out we took the same subway. She got off at Seventy-second Street. . . . To make a long story short, I got a seat next to her one day and we started talking.

TIMMY. That's it?

JOHN. Yes.

TIMMY. Sounds like an ordinary pick up to me.

JOHN. *Well, it wasn't* . . . I left some things out.

TIMMY. Such as?

JOHN. I don't remember. . . . It was twenty-five years ago.

TIMMY. The way I heard it, you followed her for a month before you finally got the nerve to speak.

JOHN. I thought you didn't know the story.

TIMMY. To convince her your intentions were honorable you asked if you might call at her home. True or false? . . . Well?

JOHN. True. (*Chuckles.*) You wouldn't believe how nervous I was. And she didn't make it any easier. . . . Pretended the whole thing was a complete surprise. Bernhardt couldn't have done it nicer. . . . Or looked nicer. . . . All in blue. . . . Blue dress, blue hat, blue shoes. . . . Everything blue. . . . Light blue. . . . And dignified. . . . One look at her you knew she was a lady. . . . My family *called* her *The Lady.* To their minds it was an insult. (*Looks at* TIMMY.) How did we get on this?

TIMMY. You were—

(*He is interrupted by the opening of the outside door.* NETTIE *enters.*)

JOHN. Join the party.

(*She enters the kitchen.*)

TIMMY. We're having a little hair of the dog.

NETTIE. How was the game? (*Puts gloves and bag on counter.*)

JOHN. One-sided.

TIMMY. Pop was just telling me how you and he met.

(NETTIE *turns to* JOHN *questioningly.*)

JOHN. He asked me.

TIMMY. (*To his mother, indicating his father.*) His version is a little different from yours.

NETTIE. What do you mean? (*Takes off her coat.*)

TIMMY. He says *you* chased *him.*

NETTIE. That'll be the day.

TIMMY. Says you did everything but stand on your head to attract his attention. (NETTIE *is not sure now whether he's kidding or not.*) That's what he said.

(NETTIE *looks uncertainly from* TIMMY *to* JOHN. *They break up simultaneously.*)

NETTIE. You two. (*Hangs up coat and bag in closet.*)

JOHN. How about a beer? (*Gets beer from refrigerator and glass from shelf.*)

NETTIE. No, thanks.

JOHN. Come on— TIMMY. Be a sport.

NETTIE. All right.

JOHN. That a girl. (*Crosses* D. *to* L. *of table; opens beer and pours.*)

NETTIE. Just a glass. (*To* TIMMY, *while* JOHN *gets the beer, crossing between them.*) What *did* he tell you?

TIMMY. He said you were dressed in blue and nobody ever looked nicer.

NETTIE. I'll bet.

TIMMY. (*To* JOHN.) Didn't you say that?

JOHN. I'm a stranger here.

NETTIE. Did he tell you how he used his friend Eddie Barnes?

JOHN. Bless us and save us.

NETTIE. Every night they'd get on the subway; stand right in front of me; and have a loud conversation about how well they were doing in business.

JOHN. It wasn't every night.

NETTIE. Poor Eddie had to go an hour out of his way.

TIMMY. That's what I call a friend. (*Crosses to chair* C. NETTIE *crosses* R., *sees roses.*)

JOHN. The best I ever had. (*Extends a glass of beer to* NETTIE.) Here you go. (*She stares.*) Here's your beer.

(*She continues looking off. He follows her gaze to the roses.*)

NETTIE. Where did they come from?

TIMMY. Pop got them . . . for you. (*Sits.*)

NETTIE. (*To* JOHN.) You did?

JOHN. Yes. (*Sits.*)

NETTIE. (*She goes to the roses.*) They're beautiful. . . . Thank you.

JOHN. You're welcome.

NETTIE. What made you do it?

JOHN. We happened to pass a place and I know you like them.

NETTIE. I haven't had red roses since Papa died. (*To* TIMMY.) He used to send me a dozen on my birthday. Never missed.

TIMMY. I remember.

NETTIE. (*To* JOHN.) Thank you.

JOHN. You're welcome.

NETTIE. I'm going to cry. (*She does.*)

JOHN. You don't bring flowers—they cry. You do—they cry.

NETTIE. I'm sorry.

TIMMY. What's to be sorry?

NETTIE. He was the kindest, gentlest man that ever lived.

TIMMY. I know.

NETTIE. (*Turns* L.) I'm all right now.

JOHN. (*Handing her the glass of beer.*) Here's what you need.

NETTIE. Maybe so. (*Takes glass.*)

TIMMY. (*Rises; raising his beer.*) To happy days.

JOHN AND NETTIE. (*As* JOHN *rises.*) To happy days.

(*All drink.*)

NETTIE. (*Crosses to roses and looks at them.*) They're just beautiful.

JOHN. (*As he and* TIMMY *sit; anxious to change the subject.*) Talking of Eddie Barnes before, God rest his soul, reminds me of the time Old Emerson put up a second hand car for the man who sold the most coffee over a three-month period. I won it but couldn't drive. Eddie said he'd teach me. We didn't get two blocks from the office when he ran broadside into an ice truck.

NETTIE. (*Sits.*) How about that ride to Connecticut? He practically killed us all.

JOHN. What was the name of the place we stayed at?

NETTIE. The Rainbow Grove.

JOHN. That's right. Big fat red-haired dame ran it.

NETTIE. Mrs. Hanlon.

JOHN. (*Mimicking Mrs. Hanlon a la Mae West.*) "My friends all call me Daisy." (*He and* NETTIE *laugh.*) I dubbed her the Will Rogers of Connecticut—She never met a man she didn't like. (*All laugh.*)

NETTIE. Remember the night you, Eddie, and a couple of others picked her up, bed and all and left her sleeping in the middle of the baseball field?

JOHN. In the morning when we went out to play, she was still there.

TIMMY. What did you do?

JOHN. We ruled that any ball hitting her on the fly was a ground-rule double. (*All laugh.*) We had a lot of fun at that place.

NETTIE. Yes.

JOHN. I wonder if it's still there.

NETTIE. I wonder.

JOHN. Let's take a ride some day and see.

NETTIE. All right. (*She starts to rise.*)

JOHN. Where you going?

NETTIE. (*Crosses to sink with glass.*) Have to start supper.

JOHN. (*Rises.*) Forget it—we're eating out!

NETTIE. I bought a steak.

JOHN. It'll keep. (*To* TIMMY.) Where would you like to go, Champ?

(TIMMY *rises and crosses* L.)

NETTIE. Maybe he has a date.

JOHN. Bring her along.

TIMMY. I don't have a date.

NETTIE. (*Crossing to between them.*) I thought you'd be seeing that Davis girl?

TIMMY. That's finished.

NETTIE. She was a nice girl.

JOHN. She was a dunce.

NETTIE. John!

TIMMY. Pop's right.

NETTIE. You men are terrible.

TIMMY. You're too kind.

JOHN. Well, where are we going?

TIMMY. You two settle it while I see a man about a dog. (*He exits through living room and* U. L.)

JOHN. How about the Concourse Plaza? (*At doorway.*)

NETTIE. (*During the following, she clears table, throws beer cans under sink.*) All right.

JOHN. (*Crosses* D. L.) I had a nice day today.

NETTIE. I'm glad.

JOHN. He's quite a boy.

NETTIE. That's what I've been telling you for years.

JOHN. We talked about things. Really talked. The way Eddie and I used to. . . . (*Crosses* U.) The hell with the Concourse Plaza! Let's go downtown! (*Crosses* R.) Let's go to the New Yorker!

NETTIE. You *are* in a good mood.

JOHN. Because I want to go downtown?

NETTIE. That and the roses.

JOHN. (*Crosses* D. *to* L. *of table.*) Are you going to talk about those roses all night?

NETTIE. I just wanted to thank you for them.

JOHN. You already have.

NETTIE. You sound as though you're sorry you got them.

JOHN. (*Crosses* D. L.) Don't be ridiculous.

NETTIE. (*Two steps* D.) Then what are you angry about?

JOHN. (*Crosses* D.) I'm just tired of hearing about them. A guy gets some roses—big deal.

NETTIE. You're embarrassed.

JOHN. I am not.

NETTIE. (*Crosses* R. C.) You did something nice and you're embarrassed.

JOHN. You don't know what you're talking about.

NETTIE. Don't worry, I won't tell anyone.

JOHN. *Nettie, please.*

NETTIE. (*Crosses to his* R.) All right, but I want to let you know how much I appreciate it.

JOHN. Good. I'm glad.

NETTIE. I do . . . I really do. (*On an impulse she touches his arm. The contact is mutually startling. Flustered, she turns away.*) We haven't been to the New Yorker in years . . . (*Crosses to counter for hat and gloves.*) I wonder if they still have the ice show. . . . Do you suppose we'll have any trouble getting in on a Saturday night?

(TIMMY *enters, picking up* JOHN'S *hat from living room table.*)

TIMMY. What did you decide?

JOHN. We're going to the Hotel New Yorker.

TIMMY. Well, digga digga do. (*Tosses* JOHN *his hat.*)

JOHN. After that we're going to The Diamond Horseshoe. And then The Sawdust Trail. (*Puts on his jacket.*)

TIMMY. Sounds like our night to howl. (*Puts on his jacket.*)

JOHN. That's what it is. (*He howls.*)

TIMMY. You call that a howl?

(*He howls louder. Now* JOHN *howls. Now* TIMMY. *Now* JOHN. *Now* TIMMY. *Each howl is louder than the last as:*)

THE CURTAIN DESCENDS

ACT ONE

SCENE 3

TIME: *Two A.M. Sunday morning.*

AT RISE: *The apartment is in darkness. From the hallway outside the apartment, we hear* TIMMY *and* JOHN *in loud but dubious harmony.*

TIMMY and JOHN. (*Offstage.*) "Farewell Piccadilly . . . Hello Leicester Square . . . It's a long, long way to Tipperary . . . But my heart's right there."

NETTIE. (*Offstage.*) You'll wake the Feldmans.

JOHN. (*Offstage.*) Nothing could wake the Feldmans.

(TIMMY *and* JOHN *laugh.*)

NETTIE. (*Offstage.*) Open the door.

JOHN. (*Offstage.*) Can't find my keys.

TIMMY. (*Offstage—giggling.*) I can't find the door.

NETTIE. (*Offstage.*) Honestly.

JOHN. (*Offstage.*) Where would you be if you were my keys?

NETTIE. (*Offstage.*) Here—I'll do it.

JOHN. (*Offstage.*) Did you ever see such pretty hair?

NETTIE. (*Offstage.*) Stop.

TIMMY. (*Offstage.*) Beautiful hair.

NETTIE. (*Offstage.*) Will you please let me open this door?

(*A KEY turns. The door opens.* NETTIE, *followed by* JOHN *and* TIMMY, *enters; TURNS on lights.*)

JOHN. (*He is wearing* TIMMY's *hat.*) Home to wife and mother. (*Crosses* D. R. *of couch.*)

NETTIE. (*To* JOHN.) Someday we'll break our necks because you refuse to leave a light.

TIMMY. (*Crosses to* R. *of* JOHN, *singing.*) "By the light . . ." (JOHN *joins in:*) "Of the silvery moon—"

NETTIE. —That's just enough. (*Taking coat off rear chair.*)

JOHN. Whatever you say, Antoinette.

(TIMMY *tosses* JOHN's *hat on* U. S. *table.*)

NETTIE. I say to bed. (*She turns* L.)

JOHN. (*Crossing* R. *of* NETTIE.) Shank of the evening. (*He grabs her around the waist and manages a squeeze before she breaks away to* L. *with an indignant exclamation. Ignoring the look of censure she directs at him, he turns to* TIMMY.) No sir, you can't beat a law degree. Springboard for anything.

TIMMY. So they say.

NETTIE. (*To* JOHN.) Anyone can be a lawyer. How many people become writers?

JOHN. (*To her.*) That's my point.

NETTIE. You should be proud to have a son who wants to try something different.

JOHN. Did I say I wasn't proud of him?

TIMMY. Abra ka dabra ka deedra slatter-in. (*They regard him.*) The fellow in the red jacket who leads the horses to the post at Jamaica always says that when they reach the starting gate. Abra ka dabra ka deedra slatter-in. And here are your horses for the fifth race. . . . Long as you can say it, you're not drunk. . . . *Abra ka dabra ka deedra slatter-in.*

JOHN. (*Crossing to* R. *of* TIMMY.) Abra ka dabra . . .

TIMMY. Ka deedra slatter-in.

NETTIE. Honestly. (*Puts her hat and coat and* JOHN'S *jacket in closet.*)

JOHN. Ka zebra—

TIMMY. —Not zebra. Deedra . . . Ka deedra slatter-in . . . Abra ka dabra ka deedra slatter-in.

JOHN. Abra . . . ka dabra . . . ka deedra . . . slatter-in.

TIMMY. Faster.

JOHN. (*Dancing jig.*) Abra, ka dabra, ka deedra, slatter-in.

TIMMY. Faster.

JOHN. Abra ka dabra ka deedra slatter-in.

NETTIE. (*Crosses* D. *to* L. *of couch.*) Have you both lost your minds?

JOHN. Nothing wrong with us that a little nightcap wouldn't cure. (*He enters the kitchen, hides* D. S. *of door.*)

NETTIE. (*Following him.*) I'll nightcap you. (JOHN

grabs her around waist. She breaks and crosses below table R.)

TIMMY. (*Crossing* D.) I can't bear to hear married people fight.

JOHN. (*To* NETTIE.) We ought to go dancing more.

NETTIE. (*Crosses* D. R. *of table.*) Now I know you're drunk.

TIMMY. (*Calling from the living room.*) Who was it that used to call us The Four Mortons?

JOHN. (*Calling back, crossing* D. *to chair.*) Harold Bowen.

TIMMY. (*Staring at the audience.*) I wish we were.

JOHN. (*To* NETTIE.) Remember the first dance I took you to?

NETTIE. Of course.

JOHN. I'll bet you don't.

NETTIE. Of course I do.

TIMMY. (*Lost in contemplation of audience.*) I have this magical feeling about vaudeville.

JOHN. (*To* NETTIE.) Where was it then?

NETTIE. (*Crosses* U. L. *of table.*) The Crystal Terrace.

JOHN. (*Crosses* R. *of table.*) And what was the first song?

NETTIE. It's too late for quiz games.

TIMMY. (D. C. *in living room.*) It doesn't matter how cheap and tinny the show is. . . . Soon as the house lights go down and the band starts up, I could cry.

JOHN. (*To* NETTIE.) The first song we ever danced to was "Pretty Baby." (*He hums a bit of the melody.*) A blond guy crooned it.

NETTIE. Through a gold megaphone.

JOHN. You *do* remember.

NETTIE. Of course. (*She crosses into living room.* JOHN *crosses to her. To escape his overture, she sits on couch arm.*)

TIMMY. (*To the audience—a la Smith and Dale.*) "I've got snew in my blood." . . . "What's snew?" . . . "Nothing. What's snew with you?" (*Crosses* L.)

NETTIE. (*To* JOHN—*indicating* TIMMY.) What's he doing?

JOHN. Playing the Palace. (*Crosses* D. R.)

TIMMY. (*To the audience as he takes off his jacket.*) "Take off the coat my boy . . . Take . . . off . . . the . . . coat . . . Tay-ake . . . o-f-f-f-f . . . the coat-t-t-t-t."

JOHN and TIMMY. (*Sing.*) "The coat is off." (TIMMY *puts his jacket on chair.*)

NETTIE. (*To* TIMMY.) Will you please go to bed?

TIMMY. (*To the audience.*) In closing I would like to do a dance made famous by the inimitable Pat Rooney. (*Nods to* JOHN.) Maestro, if you please.

(JOHN *begins to hum "The Daughter of Rosie O'Grady" as both he and* TIMMY *dance in the manner of Pat Rooney.*)

NETTIE. John! Timmy! (*They stop dancing.*) Mama expects us at twelve.

TIMMY. (*To the audience.*) We're running a bit long, folks: No dance tonight. My mother thanks you. My father thanks you. My sister thanks you. And the Feldmans thank you. (*He goes into Jimmy Durante's closing song.*) "Good night . . . Good night . . . Good night—"

NETTIE. —*Good night.*

TIMMY. (*Kisses* NETTIE.) Good night, Mrs. Cleary—whoever you are.

NETTIE. Good night, dear.

TIMMY. (*To* JOHN—*indicating the audience.*) Tough house but I warmed them up for you.

JOHN. (*Shakes hand.*) Thanks.

TIMMY. Don't look now, but your leg's broken.

JOHN. (*Limps* L. *as* NETTIE *crosses to coffee table.*) The show must go on.

TIMMY. (*To* NETTIE—*indicating* JOHN.) Plucky lad. (*Extends his hand to* JOHN.) Honor to share the bill with you.

JOHN. (*Shaking with him.*) Likewise.

TIMMY. Sleep well, chaps.

JOHN. Night, Champ.

NETTIE. Sure you don't want an alka seltzer?

TIMMY. Abra ka dabra ka deedra slatter-in . . . see you in the morning.

JOHN. With the help of God.

TIMMY. (*Moving toward his room.*) Abra ka dabra ka deedra slatter-in . . . Abra ka dabra ka deedra slatter-in. . . . And here are your horses for . . . (*Enters his room; closes the door.*)

NETTIE. Home two days and both nights to bed like that.

JOHN. He's entitled. You should hear some of the things he's been through. They overran one of those concentration camps—

NETTIE. —I don't want to hear about it now.

JOHN. (*Crosses to her* L.) You're right. It's no way to end a happy evening.

NETTIE. I think we have some aspirin in the kitchen. (*She moves into the kitchen. He follows; watches her take a bottle of aspirin from counter drawer.*)

JOHN. (*Crossing to kitchen table.*) You didn't say anything before about a headache.

NETTIE. I don't have a headache.

JOHN. Then what—

NETTIE. —I read that if you put an aspirin in cut flowers they keep longer. (*She drops an aspirin in the vase; regards the roses.*) I wonder what made you get them?

JOHN. I don't know.

NETTIE. There must have been some reason. (*Smells them.*)

JOHN. I just thought it would be nice to do.

NETTIE. (*She turns to him.*) It was.

(*They regard each other a moment.*)

JOHN. I like your dress.

NETTIE. (*Crosses to counter with aspirin bottle.*) You've seen it before.

JOHN. (*Crossing to above her.*) It looks different. . . . Everything about you looks different.

NETTIE. (*Turns to him.*) What mass are you going to?

JOHN. Ten o'clock.

NETTIE. (*Picking up the vase of roses and starting toward the living room.*) I better set the alarm.

JOHN. Nettie? (*She turns to him.*) I had a good time tonight.

NETTIE. So did I. (NETTIE *enters the living room and places the roses on coffee table; arranges them.*)

JOHN. (*Following her into the living room, to* L. *of phone.*) Did you really? Or were you putting it on for his sake?

NETTIE. I really did.

JOHN. (*Crosses to her* R.) So did I.

NETTIE. (*Crosses to chair and picks up* TIMMY'S *jacket.*) I'll set the alarm for nine-fifteen. (*She starts away again.*)

JOHN. Now that he's back we'll have lots of good times.

NETTIE. (*She stops.*) What's wrong between you and I has nothing to do with him.

JOHN. (*Crosses to her* L.) I didn't say it did.

NETTIE. We have to solve our own problems.

JOHN. (*Crosses to her* R.) Of course.

NETTIE. They can't be solved in one night.

JOHN. (*Takes jacket from her and puts it on chair.*) I know.

NETTIE. (*She crosses to* C.) One nice evening doesn't make everything different.

JOHN. (*Crosses with her and puts his arms around her waist.*) Did I say it did? (*His lips brush the nape of her neck.*)

NETTIE. I guess you don't understand.

JOHN. (*Kisses her neck.*) I forgot how nice you smelled.

NETTIE. You'll spoil everything.

JOHN. (*Squeezes her waist.*) I want things right between us.

NETTIE. You think this is going to make them right?

JOHN. (*His hands moving to her breasts.*) We have to start someplace.

NETTIE. (*Breaking away* R.) *Start?*

JOHN. Bless us and save us.

NETTIE. *That's not my idea of a start.*

JOHN. Nettie, I want you . . . I want you like I never wanted anything in my life.

NETTIE. (*Covering her ears.*) Stop.

JOHN. (*Crosses to her* L.) *Please?*

NETTIE. (*Crosses to chair, picks up* TIMMY'S *jacket and crosses to* L. *of couch.*) You're drunk.

JOHN. (*Turns* L.) *Do you think I could ask again if I wasn't?*

NETTIE. I'm not one of your hotel lobby whores.

JOHN. If you were I wouldn't have to ask.

NETTIE. A couple of drinks, a couple of jokes, and let's jump in bed.

JOHN. Maybe that's my mistake.

NETTIE. How do you suppose Ruskin managed without you today? (*Crosses* U.)

JOHN. (*Follows to her* L.) Maybe you don't want to be asked! (*He seizes her.*)

NETTIE. Let me alone.

JOHN. (*As they struggle at couch.*) *You've had the drinks! You've had the jokes!*

NETTIE. *Stop!* (*She breaks free of him, regards him for a moment, then picks up the vase of roses and hurls them against the floor. The impact is shattering. They both freeze. For a moment there is silence. Now* TIMMY'S *door opens.*)

TIMMY. (*Entering.*) What happened?

NETTIE. The roses . . . I knocked them over.

TIMMY. Sounded like a bomb.

NETTIE. I'm sorry I woke you. (TIMMY *bends to pick up a piece of the vase.*) Don't . . . I'll clean up. You go back to bed. (*He hesitates.*) Please.

TIMMY. (*Puts pieces of vase on coffee table.*) All right. . . . Good night.

NETTIE. Good night.
TIMMY. Good night, Pop.

(JOHN, *his back to* TIMMY, *remains silent.* TIMMY *hesitates a moment then goes off to his room: closes his door.*)

NETTIE. (*To* JOHN.) You moved me this afternoon. . . . When you brought the roses, I felt something stir I thought was dead forever. (*Regards the roses on the floor.*) And now this. . . . I don't understand.

JOHN. (*Without turning.*) I had nothing to do with the roses. . . . They were *his* idea.

(*As she bends and starts to pick up the roses there is a:*)

SLOW CURTAIN

END OF ACT ONE

ACT TWO

SCENE 1

TIME: *Nine-fifteen A.M. Sunday morning.*

AT RISE: JOHN *and* NETTIE *are at the breakfast table, in silence. Both face front.*

JOHN. (*Slams cup down.*) Coffee's weak.
NETTIE. Add water.
JOHN. I said *weak*. . . . Waste of time bringing good coffee into this house. . . . (*He looks for a reaction. She offers none.*) I'm thinking about renting the lake house this summer. . . . (*Still no reaction from her.*) Business is off. . . . (*Still no reaction.*) Well, what do you say?
NETTIE. About what?
JOHN. Renting the lake house.
NETTIE. Timmy will be disappointed.
JOHN. How about you?
NETTIE. I'm in favor of it.
JOHN. Of course you are.
NETTIE. I wonder why.

(TIMMY *enters from his bedroom and crosses to kitchen.*)

TIMMY. (*Crossing to* NETTIE.) Morning.
NETTIE. Good morning.
TIMMY. (*He kisses her. To* JOHN.) Morning.
JOHN. Nice of you to join us.
TIMMY. My pleasure.
JOHN. This isn't a hotel. We have our meals at certain times.
TIMMY. (*He now senses his father's irritation.*) You should have woke me.
NETTIE. (*To* TIMMY.) It's all right.

JOHN. Of course it is.

NETTIE. (*To* TIMMY, *who regards his father puzzledly.*) Sit down. (TIMMY *sits.*) What do you want?

TIMMY. Coffee.

NETTIE. Just coffee?

TIMMY. Stomach's a bit shaky.

NETTIE. You should have taken that alka seltzer. (*Rises and crosses to stove for coffee.*)

TIMMY. I'll be all right.

(NETTIE *pours coffee for* JOHN *and* TIMMY, *then returns pot to stove.*)

JOHN. Two days—two hangovers. Is that what they taught you in the Army?

TIMMY. (*To* JOHN.) Cream, please? (JOHN *passes the cream, banging it.*) Thank you.

JOHN. I'm thinking of renting the lake house.

TIMMY. How come?

JOHN. I can use the money.

TIMMY. Oh. . . .

JOHN. That all you're going to say?

TIMMY. What do you expect me to say?

JOHN. I thought that house meant something to you.

TIMMY. It does. But if you need the money—

JOHN. —A bunch of strangers sleeping in our beds, using our things—doesn't bother you at all?

TIMMY. If it has to be it has to be.

JOHN. Of course! I forgot! What's a little summer cottage, after the earth-shattering things you've been through?

TIMMY. (*To* NETTIE—*holding up the cream pitcher.*) Do you have more cream?

NETTIE. (*Taking the pitcher to refrigerator.*) Yes.

JOHN. What do you want more cream for?

TIMMY. Coffee's strong.

JOHN. It's weak.

TIMMY. It's too strong for me. (NETTIE *returns the refilled pitcher to him, then sits at table.*) Thanks. (*Adds cream to his coffee.*)

JOHN. A few months in the army and they're experts on everything. Even coffee.

TIMMY. Who said that?

JOHN. By the time I was your age I was in the coffee business nine years. . . . Nine years. . . . When I was seventeen they sent me to Brazil for three months.

TIMMY. I know.

JOHN. I'd never even been out of New York before but I went down there on my own and did my job.

TIMMY. For Emerson, wasn't it?

JOHN. No uniform. No buddies. No Uncle Sam to lean on. Just myself. . . . All alone in that strange place.

TIMMY. That's the time you grew the moustache to look older.

JOHN. Who's telling the story?

TIMMY. Sorry.

JOHN. Thirty-five years in the business and *he's* going to tell me about coffee.

TIMMY. I wasn't telling you anything about anything. I just said that for me, the coffee was too strong.

JOHN. It isn't strong!

TIMMY. (*To* NETTIE.) What time's dinner?

NETTIE. Mama expects us at twelve.

JOHN. I suppose you'll wear your uniform.

TIMMY. It's the only thing I have that fits.

JOHN. Are you sure? I mean maybe you haven't grown as much as you think.

TIMMY. (*Studiously trying to avoid a fight, he turns to* NETTIE.) Ravioli?

NETTIE. And meat balls.

JOHN. G.I. Bill, Home Loans, discharge bonus, unemployment insurance— You boys did pretty well for yourselves.

NETTIE. They did pretty well for us, too.

JOHN. (*Sings.*) "Oh, say can you see. . . ."

TIMMY. What's your point, Pop?

JOHN. The war's over.

TIMMY. I'll buy that.

JOHN. The world doesn't owe anyone a living—including veterans.

TIMMY. I'll buy that too.

JOHN. Let the Jews support you.

TIMMY. Come again?

JOHN. Wasn't for them we wouldn't have gotten in it in the first place.

TIMMY. I thought you broke that record.

JOHN. Lousy kikes.

NETTIE. John!

TIMMY. (*To* NETTIE.) I changed my mind—I'll have some toast.

JOHN. (*To* TIMMY.) Don't tell me you've lost your great love for the Jews?

NETTIE. *Stop it!* (*Rises and crosses to counter.*)

TIMMY. (*To* NETTIE.) It's all right.

JOHN. How nice of you to let me talk in my own house. And me not even a veteran.

(NETTIE *puts bread in toaster.*)

TIMMY. Would you mind telling me what you're mad about?

JOHN. Who's mad?

NETTIE. (*To* TIMMY.) Anything on the toast?

TIMMY. Honey, if you've got it.

JOHN. A man states a few facts and right away he's mad.

NETTIE. (*At window.*) How about strawberry jam?

TIMMY. No.

JOHN. If I get a half-way decent offer I might sell the lake house.

NETTIE. Peach?

TIMMY. All right.

JOHN. (*He rises and crosses to counter for toothpick, as* NETTIE *gets plate from cupboard.*) Hurry up with your breakfast.

TIMMY. What for?

JOHN. Mass starts in twenty minutes and you're not even dressed.

TIMMY. Mass?

JOHN. Mass.

TIMMY. I haven't been to mass in over two years. You know that.

JOHN. (*Crosses to* L. *of table.*) Lots of bad habits you boys picked up that you'll have to get over.

TIMMY. Not going to mass isn't a habit I picked up. It's a decision I came to after a lot of thought.

JOHN. (*Crosses to* TIMMY.) What way is that for a Catholic to talk?

TIMMY. I haven't considered myself a Catholic for quite a while.

JOHN. (*Crosses* D. L.) Must be something wrong with my ears.

NETTIE. (*Gets toast from toaster, crosses to table with it and sits. To* JOHN.) You knew this was coming. Why pretend it's such a shock?

JOHN. Now there's a familiar alliance. (*To* TIMMY.) So you've outgrown the faith?

TIMMY. It doesn't answer my needs.

JOHN. Outgrown your old clothes and outgrown the faith.

TIMMY. Pop, will you listen to me—?

JOHN. —Billions of people have believed in it since the beginning of time but it's not good enough for you.

TIMMY. It's not a question of good enough.

JOHN. What do you say when people ask what religion you are?

TIMMY. Nothing.

JOHN. You say you're nothing?

TIMMY. Yes.

JOHN. The Clearys have been Catholics since . . . since the beginning of time. And now you, a Cleary, are going to tell people that you're nothing?

TIMMY. Yes.

JOHN. *You're an atheist!* (*Crosses* D.)

NETTIE. John!

JOHN. (*Crosses* U.) When you come to the blank after religion on those college applications, put down atheist.

(*Crosses* D.) Make a big hit in those Ivy League places, from what I hear.

TIMMY. I'm not an atheist.

JOHN. (*Crosses* U.) Then what are you?

TIMMY. I don't know. . . . But I'd like a chance to find out.

JOHN. You don't know what you believe in?

TIMMY. Do *you?*

JOHN. Yes.

TIMMY. Tell me. . . . Well, go on!

JOHN. I believe in the Father, the Son and the Holy Ghost. . . . I believe that God created man in his own image. . . . I—

TIMMY. —Pop, look. . . . If your faith works for you I'm glad. I'm very glad. I wish it worked for me. . . . But it doesn't.

JOHN. Do you believe in God—yes or no?

TIMMY. I don't believe in Heaven, or Hell, or Purgatory, or—

JOHN. —*Yes or no?*

TIMMY. I believe there's something bigger than myself. What you call it or what it is I don't know.

JOHN. (*Crosses* D. L.) Well, this is a fine how do you do!

NETTIE. (*To* JOHN.) Yesterday you said he was a man. A man has a right to decide such things for himself.

JOHN. "Good morning, Father Riley." "Good morning, Mr. Cleary. I understand your boy's out of service." "Yes, Father." "Where is he this fine Sunday morning, Mr. Cleary?" "Home, Father." "Is he sick, Mr. Cleary?" "No, Father." "Then why isn't he here in church, Mr. Cleary?" "He's become an atheist, Father."

TIMMY. I'm not an atheist!

JOHN. (*Crossing* U. *to* TIMMY.) Whatever you are, I won't have it! I'm the boss of this house. If you want to go on living here you'll do as I say. And I say you're going to church with me this morning.

NETTIE. (*To* JOHN.) *Do you know what you're doing?*

JOHN. (*To* NETTIE.) Keep out! (*To* TIMMY.) Well?

NETTIE. (*Rises; to* TIMMY.) Don't pay any attention to him.

TIMMY. (*Rises; to* NETTIE.) It's all right. (*To* JOHN.) I'll go to church with you. Be out in a minute. (*Starts into living room.*)

JOHN. Forget it!

TIMMY. (*At his bedroom door, turns.*) What?

JOHN. I said forget it. The Lord doesn't want anybody in His house who has to be dragged there. (*To* NETTIE.) Score another one for your side.

TIMMY. It has nothing to do with her.

JOHN. (*To* TIMMY *as he crosses to closet.*) Wait till you're down on all fours some day— You'll be glad to see a priest then.

NETTIE. We'll meet you at Mama's.

JOHN. (*Putting on jacket and hat.*) I won't be there.

NETTIE. She expects us.

JOHN. We all have our disappointments.

TIMMY. I said I'd go with you.

(JOHN *exits—slamming the door.*)

NETTIE. Now, what was that all about? (*Sits at kitchen table.*)

TIMMY. (*Furious with himself; crossing to kitchen.*) I should have gone with him.

NETTIE. I'll never understand that man.

TIMMY. Why didn't I just go? Why did I have to make an issue?

NETTIE. It wasn't your fault.

TIMMY. It never *is*.

NETTIE. When he's in one of those moods there's nothing anyone can do.

TIMMY. (*Crosses* D. L. *of table.*) The alliance, he called us.

NETTIE. Everyone's entitled to their own beliefs.

TIMMY. That's what we must seem like to him—an alliance. Always two against one. Always us against him. . . . Why?

NETTIE. If you're through eating, I'll clear the table.

TIMMY. Didn't you hear me?

NETTIE. Evidently, your father's not the only one who got up on the wrong side of the bed this morning.

TIMMY. *I'm not talking about this morning.*

NETTIE. There's no need to shout.

TIMMY. (*Crosses* U.) You, and him, and me, and what's been going on here for twenty years. . . . It's got to stop.

NETTIE. What's got to stop?

TIMMY. *We've* got to stop ganging up on him.

NETTIE. Is that what we've been doing?

TIMMY. You said you've never understood him.

NETTIE. And never will.

TIMMY. Have you ever really tried? . . .

NETTIE. Go on.

TIMMY. Have you ever tried to see things from his point of view?

NETTIE. What things?

TIMMY. The lake house, for instance.

NETTIE. The lake house?

TIMMY. It's the pride and joy of his life and you're always knocking it.

NETTIE. Do you know why?

TIMMY. Because he bought it without consulting you.

NETTIE. Drove me out to this God-forsaken lake. Pointed to a bungalow with no heat or hot water and said, "That's where we'll be spending our summers from now on." (*Rises, clears table, covers toaster.*)

TIMMY. An hour's ride from New York City isn't exactly God-forsaken.

NETTIE. It wasn't an hour's ride twenty years ago.

TIMMY. The point is would he have gotten it any other way? If he had come to you and said he wanted to buy a cottage on a lake in New Jersey, would you have said yes?

NETTIE. (*Crossing to* R. *chair.*) I might have.

TIMMY. No. Not if it had been a palace with fifty servants.

NETTIE. I don't like the country.

TIMMY. We'd have spent every summer right here.

NETTIE. My idea of a vacation is to travel—see something new.

TIMMY. You had a chance to see Brazil.

NETTIE. That was different.

TIMMY. The fellow who took that job is a millionaire today.

NETTIE. And still living in Brazil.

TIMMY. Which is not to be compared with the Bronx.

NETTIE. So it's my fault we're not millionaires.

TIMMY. Your mother might have loved Brazil! (*This causes her to turn from him.*) You violently objected to moving from Yorkville to the Bronx. . . . Why?

NETTIE. (*Putting dirty dishes in sink.*) I hate the Bronx.

TIMMY. (*Pursuing her.*) But you insisted that your mother move up here.

NETTIE. They tore down her building. She had to move somewhere. (*She goes to pick up the last cup remaining on the table.* TIMMY *beats her to it, holds the cup and her attention.*)

TIMMY. Except for summers at the lake, have you ever gone two days without seeing her?

NETTIE. Only because of Willis. (TIMMY *gives her the cup and crosses to living room,* L. *of couch; she follows to* R. *of couch with cup.*) Where are you going?

TIMMY. To get dressed. Then I'm going to church and apologize to him for acting like a fool.

NETTIE. You'll be at Mama's for dinner?

TIMMY. Only if he'll come with me.

NETTIE. You disappointed Willis yesterday. You can't do it again.

TIMMY. Oh yes I can!

NETTIE. How cruel. (*Crosses, puts cup in sink, then to counter.*)

TIMMY. Cruel! (*Crosses* L. *of kitchen table.*) Not as cruel as your dragging me over there every day when I was little. And when I was bigger, and couldn't go every day, concentrating on Sunday. "Is it too much to give your crippled cousin one day a week?" (*Crosses* R. *of table.*) And when I didn't go there on Sunday, I felt so guilty that I couldn't enjoy myself anyway. . . . I hate Sunday, and I don't think I'll ever get over it. But I'm going to try.

NETTIE. (*Crosses* D.) How fortunate for the cripples in this world that everyone isn't as selfish as you.

TIMMY. Why do you keep calling him a cripple? That's not the worst thing wrong with Willis. It's his mind. He's like a four year old.

NETTIE. (*Turns to him.*) Can a four year old read a book?

TIMMY. (*Pressing his attack relentlessly.*) Yes, he reads. After you drilling him every day for twenty years. But does he have any idea what he's reading about? . . . If you and the rest of them over there want to throw your lives away on him, you go ahead and do it! But don't try and sacrifice me to the cause! (NETTIE, *stunned by* TIMMY'S *assault, exits from the kitchen, disappears into the bedroom. Immediately regretful at having vented his feelings so strongly,* TIMMY *moves into the living room; is pondering the best way to apologize, when* NETTIE, *carrying a pocketbook, appears; she puts pocketbook on table above couch, then takes a coat from the hall closet; puts it on.*) Where are you going? (*No answer.*) Your mother doesn't expect us till twelve. (*No answer.*) Give me a minute to dress and I'll go with you. (*No answer.*) Now look— (*As* NETTIE *reaches for her pocketbook,* TIMMY *also reaches for it in an effort to prevent her departure. He wrests it from her. As he does so, his face registers surprise.*) This is like lead. (*He opens the bag, regards the contents, looks at her puzzledly.*) You've got all your coins in here. . . . You're taking your coins. . . . What for? (*She extends her hand for the bag. He surrenders it. She gets her hat from table and moves toward the door.*) Will you please say something?

NETTIE. Thank you for the roses. (*She exits.*)

CURTAIN

ACT TWO

SCENE 2

TIME: *Ten P.M. Sunday.*

AT RISE: TIMMY, *highball glass in hand, whiskey bottle on the coffee table before him, sits on the sofa in the living room. It is plain that he has been drinking for some time.* JOHN, *cold sober, at the radio, looks at his watch; then he crosses to the apartment door,* U. C., *opens it and looks out, then slams it shut.*

TIMMY. I remember sitting here like this the night she went to have John.

JOHN. (*Crosses* D. *to phone.*) Why would she just walk out and not tell anyone where she was going?

TIMMY. I was six.

JOHN. (*Crosses* U.) Without any reason.

TIMMY. Doctor Goldman came at midnight and took her to the hospital.

JOHN. (*Crosses to radio.*) It doesn't make sense.

TIMMY. After they left, I started to cry. You did, too.

JOHN. It's not like her.

TIMMY. I asked you if you loved her. You nodded. I asked you to say it. You hesitated. I got hysterical. To quiet me you finally said "I love her."

JOHN. (*Crosses to phone and lifts receiver.*) Maybe she's at Sophie's.

TIMMY. No. (JOHN *regards him questioningly.*) I called Sophie.

JOHN. (*Looking at watch.*) It's after ten.

TIMMY. I called everybody.

JOHN. (*Crosses* U. *to apartment door.*) She's been gone twelve hours.

TIMMY. They all said they'd call back if they heard from her.

JOHN. (*Crosses* D.) If she's not here by eleven o'clock I'm calling the police.

TIMMY. I wonder what difference it would have made if John lived.

JOHN. (*Crosses* L.) I wonder what department you call.

TIMMY. I remember you and I going to visit her at the hospital on a Sunday afternoon. I had to wait downstairs. First time I ever heard the word incubator. . . . Incubator.

JOHN. (*Crosses to chair and sits.*) I guess you call Missing Persons. (*Picks up newspaper.*)

TIMMY. As we left the hospital and started down the Concourse, we ran into an exotic Spanish-looking woman whom you'd met on one of your trips to Brazil. (*Rises and crosses to* JOHN.) She was a dancer. Very beautiful. You and she spoke awhile and then you and I went to a movie. Fred Astaire and Ginger Rogers in "Flying Down to Rio."

JOHN. (*Throws down paper, rises and crosses* U.) What are you talking about?

TIMMY. I always thought that was a coincidence— Meeting a South American woman and then seeing a picture about Rio. . . . *Was* it a coincidence?

JOHN. What?

TIMMY. (*Sings, crossing* D. R.) "Hey Rio, Rio by the sea-o. Got to get to Rio and I've got to make time."

JOHN. (*Crosses to* L. *of* TIMMY.) You're drunk.

TIMMY. Abra ka dabra ka deedra slatter-in.

JOHN. Fine time you picked for it.

TIMMY. A bunch of chorus girls stood on the wings of a silver plane singing that song— "Hey Rio. Flying down to Rio—"

JOHN. —You're the last one who saw her. The police will want to question you.

TIMMY. She left the house at ten A.M., Your Honor. Didn't say boo but I assumed she was going to her mother's. Brown coat. Brown hat. When I got to her mother's, she wasn't there. They hadn't seen her—hadn't heard from her. I had two helpings of ravioli and meat balls. Came back here to wait. When she didn't call by three o'clock I started to worry—

JOHN. (*Crosses above sofa.*) —And drink.

TIMMY. *When she didn't call by three o'clock I started to worry.* . . . I tried to get in touch with my father. (*Crosses to window* D. L.) Called all the bars I could think of— "Is Mr. Cleary there?" . . . "If he comes in would you please tell him to call his house?" . . . It was like old times. (*Crosses to* R. *of* JOHN.)

JOHN. (*Crosses* R.) I told you—I had dinner and went to a movie.

TIMMY. "*Is* Mr. Cleary there?"—Shows how long I've been away. (*Crosses* D.) You never say "*Is* Mr. Cleary there?" You say "Let me speak to Mr. Cleary." As though you *knew* he was there.

JOHN. I was at a movie.

TIMMY. Did it have a happy ending?

JOHN. (*Crosses* U.) "Gilda" with Rita Hayworth and Glenn Ford.

TIMMY. I didn't ask you what it was.

JOHN. At the Loew's Paradise.

TIMMY. (*Crosses to phone.*) *I didn't ask you what it was!*

JOHN. What's the matter with you?

TIMMY. (*Crossing to table for bottle.*) Join me?

JOHN. (*Crosses* D.) No, and I think you've had enough.

TIMMY. (*Picks up bottle.*) First time I ever saw you refuse a drink.

JOHN. (*Crossing to* R. *of* TIMMY.) I want you to stop.

TIMMY. (*Sits sofa, pours.*) But you're powerless to stop me. It's a lousy position to be in, *I* know.

JOHN. That's your last one. (*He starts to remove the bottle.*)

TIMMY. Take it and I leave!

(JOHN *hesitates; puts the bottle down on coffee table.*)

JOHN. Joy, joy said Mrs. Malloy. (*Crosses to phone.*)

TIMMY. Louder, louder said Mrs. . . . What rhymes with louder?

JOHN. You were sick Friday night. Sick last night. (*The PHONE rings. By the time* TIMMY *gets to his feet* JOHN *is picking up the receiver. On the phone.*) Hello? . . . Oh . . . (*The abrupt disinterest in his voice causes* TIMMY *to sit down.*) Nothing. . . . I said we haven't heard anything. . . . I know how long she's been gone. . . . Of course I'm concerned. . . . *I don't care how I sound—I'm concerned.* . . . If she's not here by eleven, that's what I'm going to do. . . . That's a comforting bit of information. (*He hangs up and crosses* D.) Her mother again. Wanted to let me know how many muggings there's been lately. (*Crosses* U.)

TIMMY. I've got it! Earl Browder.

JOHN. What?

TIMMY. Louder, louder said Mrs. Earl Browder.

JOHN. I'm glad you can take the whole thing so calmly.

TIMMY. To quote a famous authority: "I don't care how I sound—I'm concerned."

JOHN. (*Regards his watch.*) Ten after ten.

TIMMY. Trouble with you is you haven't had enough experience in these matters.

JOHN. Where the devil can she be?

TIMMY. I'm an old hand.

JOHN. Never done anything like this before in her life.

TIMMY. All those nights I lay in bed waiting for your key to turn in the door: Part of me praying you'd come home safe; part of me dreading the sound of that key because I knew there'd be a fight.

JOHN. (*Pacing.*) I'll give her a few minutes more.

TIMMY. All those mornings I woke up sick. Had to miss school. The boy's delicate, everyone said; has a weak constitution.

JOHN. I'll give her till half-past.

TIMMY. From the day I left this house I was never sick. Not once. Took me a long time to see the connection.

JOHN. (*Pacing.*) Where can she go? She has no money.

TIMMY. Wrong.

JOHN. What? (*Crossing to* TIMMY.) You said "wrong."

TIMMY. (*Rises and crosses* U.) "Hey Rio. Rio by the—"

JOHN. (*Grabs* TIMMY'S *arm.*) —I want to know what you meant.

TIMMY. She took her coins. (JOHN *goes into the bedroom.* TIMMY *crosses* D. R., *singing quietly.*) "Hey Rio. Rio by the sea-o."

JOHN. (*Re-enters, crosses* L. *of sofa.*) Why didn't you mention it before?

TIMMY. Slipped my mind.

JOHN. Over fifty dollars in dimes and quarters, and she took them all.

TIMMY. Person could go quite a ways with fifty dollars.

JOHN. You saw her take them?

TIMMY. Yes.

JOHN. Didn't it strike you as peculiar?

TIMMY. Everything strikes me as peculiar.

JOHN. There's something you're not telling me.

TIMMY. (*Crosses away from him, below coffee table.*) We all have our little secrets.

JOHN. (*Takes step toward him.*) There *is* something!

TIMMY. Take you and your money, for instance.

JOHN. I want to know what it is.

TIMMY. For all I know, we're millionaires.

JOHN. I want to know why your mother left this house!

TIMMY. Just between us chickens, how much do you have?

(TIMMY *reaches for the bottle, to pour another drink, but* JOHN *snatches it out of his reach.*)

JOHN. Answer me.

TIMMY. If you don't put that bottle down, I'm leaving.

JOHN. I want an answer!

TIMMY. (*Rising.*) See you around the pool hall.

JOHN. (*Shoving him down hard on chair* L.) *I want an answer!*

TIMMY. Hell of a way to treat a veteran. (*Reaches for bottle in* JOHN'S *hand.*)

JOHN. I've taken all the crap from you I'm going to.

TIMMY. You want an answer. I want a drink. It's a deal. (*He reaches for the bottle but* JOHN *keeps it from him.*)

JOHN. First the answer.

TIMMY. I forget the question.

JOHN. Why did your mother leave this house? . . . Well?

TIMMY. . . . We had an argument.

JOHN. About what?

TIMMY. I don't remember.

JOHN. (*A pause. He crosses* R.) Probably something to do with your drinking.

TIMMY. Yes, that's what it was. She said I drank too much.

JOHN. She's right.

TIMMY. Yes.

JOHN. (*Puts bottle on table above sofa.*) I never thought I'd see the day when you and she would argue.

TIMMY. Neither did I.

JOHN. She didn't say where she was going? Just took the coins and left?

TIMMY. That's right.

JOHN. Beats me. (*Starts toward the kitchen.*)

TIMMY. Where you going?

JOHN. To get something to eat.

TIMMY. *Eat?* (*Rises.*)

JOHN. I didn't have any supper.

TIMMY. A minute ago you were so worried you couldn't even sit down.

JOHN. I'm just going to have a sandwich.

TIMMY. Have a banquet!

JOHN. (*Crosses* D. R. *of sofa.*) What are you getting mad at *me* for? You're the one who argued with her.

TIMMY. Which absolves you completely! She might jump off a bridge but *your* conscience is clear!

JOHN. (*Crosses to* R. *of* TIMMY.) A person planning to do something like that doesn't take a bunch of change along.

TIMMY. *She thanked me for the roses!* (JOHN *just looks at him.*) Don't you have any consideration for other people's feelings?

JOHN. (*Crossing* U. R.) Consideration?

TIMMY. Don't you know how much it pleased her to think they were from you?

JOHN. (*Crossing* D. R. C.) *You* talk about consideration?

TIMMY. How could you do it?

JOHN. Do you have any idea how I looked forward to this morning? To mass, and dropping in at Rafferty's afterwards with you in your uniform?

TIMMY. Always the injured party.

JOHN. You'll be the injured party in about two minutes.

TIMMY. I already am.

JOHN. Real rough you had it. Good food. Good clothes. Always a roof over your head.

TIMMY. (*Sits chair* L.) Heigh ho, everybody, it's count your blessings time.

JOHN. I'll tell you what rough is— Being so hungry you begged. Being thrown out in the street with your few sticks of furniture for all the neighbors to enjoy. Never sleeping in a bed with less than two other people. Always hiding from collectors. Having to leave school at the age of ten because your father was crippled for life and it was your job to support the house. . . . You had it rough all right. (*Crosses* U. R.)

TIMMY. The subject was roses.

JOHN. (*Crosses* D. R.) Where I couldn't have gone with your advantages. . . . What I couldn't have been.

TIMMY. I still want to know why you told her about the roses.

JOHN. (*Pacing.*) We were having words and it slipped out.

TIMMY. Words about what? . . . Well?

JOHN. (*Pacing.*) Stop pushing or I'll tell you.

TIMMY. Go on! Go on!

JOHN. (*Crossing* C.) *The humping I'm getting is not worth the humping I'm getting.*

TIMMY. (*Rising.*) You pig.

JOHN. I'm warning you!

TIMMY. *You pig.* (JOHN'S *right hand shoots out, catches* TIMMY *hard across the side of his face.* NETTIE *enters.* JOHN *crosses to above door* D. L.) Bon soir. (NETTIE *regards them with an air of detached curiosity.*) Had one too many. . . . Lost my ka deedra slatter-in. (*Sits* L. *chair.*)

JOHN. (*Turning to her.*) Where have you been? (NETTIE *lays her pocketbook and gloves on table.*) I was about to call the police. (NETTIE *gives no indication that she even hears him.*) I want to know where you've been. (NETTIE *moves through the living room; stops in front of* TIMMY *who has just poured himself another drink.*) Are you going to tell me where you've been?

NETTIE. You wouldn't believe me.

JOHN. Of course I'd believe you.

NETTIE. (*To* TIMMY.) You don't look well.

TIMMY. Appearances are deceiving—I feel terrible.

JOHN. Why wouldn't I believe you?

NETTIE. (*Unbuttoning her coat.*) You just wouldn't.

JOHN. Tell me and see.

NETTIE. I went to the movies.

JOHN. Go on.

NETTIE. That's it. (*Hangs up coat in closet.*)

JOHN. You just went to the movies?

NETTIE. That's right. (*Sits couch.*)

JOHN. You've been gone over twelve hours.

NETTIE. I stayed for several shows.

JOHN. Are you trying to tell me you were at a movie for twelve hours?

NETTIE. I knew you wouldn't believe me.

TIMMY. *I* believe you.

NETTIE. Thank you.

TIMMY. What did you see?

NETTIE. That means you *don't* believe me.

TIMMY. No, I guess not.

JOHN. I demand to know where you were.

NETTIE. I went to the Hotel Astor; picked up a man; had a few drinks, a few jokes; went to his room and—

JOHN. —Stop it!

NETTIE. I was just getting to the best part.

JOHN. (*Turns away.*) You're making a fool of yourself.

NETTIE. Is there anything I could say that you *would* believe?

TIMMY. Say you took a bus downtown, walked around, visited a museum, had dinner, went to Radio City, and came home.

NETTIE. I took a bus downtown, walked around, visited a museum, had dinner . . .

TIMMY. Went to Radio City and came home.

NETTIE. Went to Radio City and came home.

TIMMY. I'll buy that. (*To* JOHN.) If you had any sense you'd buy it, too.

JOHN. (*Crosses* R. *below coffee table.*) I don't have any sense. I'm just a poor, ignorant slob whose wife's been missing twelve hours—and I want to know where she was.

TIMMY. What difference does it make?

JOHN. Stay out of this!

TIMMY. How?

JOHN. (*To* NETTIE.) What are you going to tell your mother?

NETTIE. Nothing.

JOHN. The poor woman's almost out of her mind.

TIMMY. There's a joke there some place.

JOHN. (*Picks up phone.*) At least call her and say you're home.

NETTIE. She'll want an explanation. When I tell her, she won't believe me any more than you did.

JOHN. I'll believe you when you tell the truth.

TIMMY. What *is* truth? (JOHN *crosses above sofa, furious.*) Sorry.

NETTIE. I'll tell you this. . . . In all my life, the past twelve hours are the only real freedom I've ever known.

TIMMY. Did you enjoy it?

NETTIE. Every moment.

TIMMY. Why did you come back?

NETTIE. I'm a coward.

JOHN. *Will somebody tell me what's going on?*

TIMMY. (*To the audience.*) You heard the question. (*He peers out into the theatre . . . points.*) Up there in the balcony. The bearded gentleman with the . . . (*He stops abruptly; rubs his stomach; regards the audience wanly.*) Sorry, folks, but I'm about to be ill.

(*He hastens off* U. L. NETTIE *follows him.* JOHN *takes advantage of her absence to examine her pocketbook; is going through it when she returns.*)

NETTIE. (*Crossing to* L. *of coffee table.*) He wouldn't let me hold his head, ordered me out of the bathroom, locked the door.

JOHN. What happened to your coins?

NETTIE. I spent them.

JOHN. How?

NETTIE. I took a bus downtown, walked around, visited a museum—

JOHN. (*He interrupts her by slamming the pocketbook to the table.*) Wasn't for his drinking, none of this would have happened.

NETTIE. Why do you say that?

JOHN. If he didn't drink, you and he wouldn't have argued. (*She regards him uncomprehendingly.*) Isn't that why you left? Because you had an argument about his drinking?

NETTIE. We had an argument, but it wasn't about drinking.

JOHN. What was it about?

NETTIE. You, mostly.

JOHN. Go on.

NETTIE. He thinks I don't give you enough credit. . . . Feels you're quite a guy. . . . Said we had to stop ganging up on you.

(JOHN *turns away.*)

CURTAIN

ACT TWO

SCENE 3

TIME: *Two A.M., Monday.*

AT RISE: *The apartment is in darkness. Now a crack of LIGHT appears beneath the door to* TIMMY'S *room. The door opens.* TIMMY, *in pajamas, emerges, goes to the living room, turns on a LAMP which reveals* NETTIE, *in nightgown and robe, sitting on the sofa.*

NETTIE. I couldn't sleep.

TIMMY. Neither could I. Came out to get a magazine.

NETTIE. You feel all right?

TIMMY. Yes. (*He looks through a pile of magazines; selects one.*)

NETTIE. What time is it?

TIMMY. Almost two. . . . Are *you* all right?

NETTIE. Yes.

TIMMY. Well, I guess I'll turn in. (*She offers no comment.*) Good night. (*Again, no response. He crosses to door* D. R.)

NETTIE. Isn't there something you want to tell me?

TIMMY. (*Turns.*) . . . As a matter of fact there is . . . but it'll keep till morning.

NETTIE. You've decided to leave.

TIMMY. Yes.

NETTIE. When?

TIMMY. (*Crosses to between sofa and chair.*) It's not a sudden decision.

NETTIE. When are you leaving?

TIMMY. In the morning. (*He looks for a comment from her, but she remains silent. He sits chair* L.) This fellow I went to high school with has a flat on Twenty-second Street. His roommate just got married and he's looking for a replacement. I figured . . . (*He becomes aware that she isn't listening.*) Hey . . . (*Still no reaction. He calls to her through rolled-up magazine.*) *Hey.* (*She regards him absently.*) Give you a penny for them.

NETTIE. An apple core.

TIMMY. What?

NETTIE. An apple core. . . . I was due to start working for a law firm. Passed all the interviews and had been notified to report for work the following Monday. . . . On Sunday, my sister and I were walking in the park when a blond boy, who had a crush on me but was too bashful to speak, demonstrated his affection by throwing an apple core which struck me here. (*She indicates the area beneath her left eye.*) When I woke up Monday morning, I had the most beautiful black eye you ever saw. Too embarrassed to start a new job looking like that, I called in sick. They called back to say the position had been filled by someone else. . . . The next job I found was the one that brought your father and I together. . . . I often think of that apple core and wonder what my life would be like if it had never been thrown.

TIMMY. Everyone wonders about things like that.

NETTIE. I was going in early to type up some dictation I'd taken the night before. . . . Front Street was deserted. . . . As I walked, I had the sensation of being watched. . . . I glanced up at the office I was passing and saw this young man, your father, staring down. . . . He regarded me intensely, almost angrily, for a moment, then suddenly realized I was looking back at him and turned away. . . . In that moment, I knew that that young man and I were not suited to each other. . . . And at the same time I knew we would become involved . . . that it was inevitable.

TIMMY. Why? You had others to choose from.

NETTIE. Oh yes. . . . All gentle, considerate men. All very much like my father. . . . One of them was the baker from Paterson, New Jersey that we always joke about.

TIMMY. The fellow who brought a hatbox full of pastries whenever he called on you.

NETTIE. Yes. . . . What a sweet man. . . . How he begged me to marry.

TIMMY. What was it that drew you to Pop?

NETTIE. I think it was his energy . . . a certain wildness. He was not like my father at all . . . I was attracted . . . and I was afraid. I've always been a little afraid of him. . . . And then he was clearly a young man who was going places. Twenty-four when I met him and making well over a hundred a week. Great money in those days and his prospects were unlimited. . . . Money was never plentiful in our house. We weren't poor like his people, you understand. Never without rent, or food, or tickets to the opera, or nice clothes. But still we weren't well to do. . . . My father brought home stories from the hotel about the various bigwigs who came in and what they wore and how they talked and acted. And we went to the opera. And we had friends who were cultured. Musical Sunday afternoons. Those were papa's happiest moments. . . . Yes, I liked good things. Things that the baker from Paterson and the others could never give me. . . . But your father surely would. The way he was going he would be a millionaire. . . . That was his dream, you know—to be a millionaire by the time he was forty. . . . Nineteen twenty-nine took care of that. He was never quite the same afterwards. . . . But when I met him he was cock of the walk. Good looking, witty young Irishman. Everyone liked him, and those who didn't at least feared him because he was a fierce fellow. Everyone wanted to go into business with him. Everyone wanted to be social with him. . . . He was immediately at home on a ship, a train . . . in any bar. Strangers thought he was magnificent. And he *was* . . . as long as the situation was impersonal. . . . At his best in an impersonal situation. . . . But that doesn't include the home, the family. . . . The baker from Paterson was all tongue-tied outside, but in the home he would have been beautiful. . . . Go to bed now.

TIMMY. (*He rises, takes her hand.*) Want the light off?

NETTIE. Please.

TIMMY. *He moves to the lamp; is about to turn it off; hesitates.*) When I left this house three years ago, I blamed *him* for everything that was wrong here. . . .

When I came home, I blamed *you*. . . . Now I suspect that no one's to blame. . . . Not even me. (*He turns the LIGHT off.*) Good night.

NETTIE. Good night. (TIMMY *exits into his room; closes the door. For a moment there is silence. Then:*) "Who loves you, Nettie?" . . . "You do, Papa." . . . "Why, Nettie?" . . . "Because I'm a nice girl, Papa."

SLOW CURTAIN

ACT TWO

SCENE 4

TIME: *Nine A.M., Monday.*

AT RISE: JOHN *and* NETTIE *are in the kitchen;* JOHN *at door;* NETTIE *at counter, getting out silver and napkins.*

JOHN. One word from you. . . . That's all it would take.

NETTIE. (*Crossing to above table.*) I'm not so sure.

JOHN. Try.

NETTIE. No.

JOHN. Do you want him to go?

NETTIE. No.

JOHN. Then say something before it's too late.

NETTIE. What do you want for breakfast?

JOHN. (*Pacing from* L. *to* R.) Who cares about breakfast?

NETTIE. Timmy's having scrambled eggs.

JOHN. *Am I the only one who's upset by what's going on here?*

NETTIE. No.

JOHN. Then how can you just stand there?

NETTIE. (*At* L. *of table.*) Would you feel better if I wept?

JOHN. You'll weep when he's gone.

NETTIE. But not now.

JOHN. (*Crossing to* R. *chair.*) All I want you to do is tell him how you feel.

NETTIE. He knows that.

JOHN. You won't speak to him?

NETTIE. (*Crossing to cupboard for cups and saucers.*) I can't.

JOHN. You're the one who'll miss him most. . . . With me it's different. I've got my business.

NETTIE. (*Crosses to table with cups and saucers.*) I envy you.

JOHN. Just ask him to wait a couple of days and think it over.

NETTIE. After a couple of days, we'd be used to having him around. It would be that much harder to see him leave.

JOHN. He might change his mind. Might not want to leave.

NETTIE. He has to leave sometime.

JOHN. But not now. Not like this.

NETTIE. Twenty-second Street isn't the end of the world.

JOHN. (*Crossing to her* R.) If he leaves this house today I don't want to see him ever again!

NETTIE. If you say that to him, make it clear that you're speaking for yourself. (*Crossing to refrigerator for cream.*)

JOHN. (*Crosses* L. *below table.*) Who's this fellow he's moving in with?

NETTIE. (*Crosses to table with cream.*) A boy he knew at high school. (*Crosses to counter and removes cover from toaster.*)

JOHN. (*Crosses* U.) Everything he wants right here—food, clothing, a room of his own. And he has to move into a dirty coldwater flat.

NETTIE. I think I understand his feeling.

JOHN. Home two days and gone again. The neighbors will have a field day.

NETTIE. (*Crosses* R. *of* JOHN.) I'm going in to call him now.

JOHN. I want to see him alone.

NETTIE. If you're wise you won't start a row.

JOHN. *I want to see him alone.*

NETTIE. . . . All right. (*She goes inside; knocks at* TIMMY'S *door.*)

TIMMY'S VOICE. Come in. (*She enters the room; closes the door after her.*)

JOHN. (*Addresses* TIMMY'S *place at the table.*) I understand you've decided to leave us . . . (*Not satisfied with this opening, he tries another; crossing* D.) What's this nonsense about your leaving? . . . (*And another; crossing* R.) Your mother tells me you're moving out. I would like to know why. (*The first part of this opening pleases him; the last part doesn't. He tries variations on it:*) I *demand* to know why. . . . Would you be so good as to tell me why? . . . *Why, God damn it?* (*He is puzzling over these various approaches when* TIMMY *enters the kitchen.*)

TIMMY. (*Crosses to* U. L. *of table.*) Good morning.

JOHN. Morning.

TIMMY. Mother said you wanted to see me.

JOHN. Sleep well?

TIMMY. Yes.

JOHN. Good. . . . (*Crosses* L.)

TIMMY. (*Crosses* U. R. *of table.*) You wanted to see me?

JOHN. Mother says you're leaving.

TIMMY. Yes.

JOHN. Rather sudden, isn't it?

TIMMY. Not really.

JOHN. Mind telling me why?

TIMMY. I just think it's best.

JOHN. For who?

TIMMY. Everyone.

JOHN. Crap! (TIMMY *starts from the room.*) *Wait.* (*The note of entreaty in his voice causes* TIMMY *to halt.* JOHN *crosses* U. L. *of him.*) I didn't mean that. . . . The fact is, I don't blame you for wanting to leave. I had no business hitting you.

TIMMY. That's not why I'm going.

JOHN. (*Crossing* D. L.) If there was any way I could undo last night, I would.

TIMMY. It's not a question of last night.

JOHN. If I had to do it over again, I'd cut my arm off.

TIMMY. Pop, listen—

JOHN. —I don't know what gets into me sometimes.

TIMMY. Pop! (JOHN *looks at him.*) I'm not leaving because of anything that happened last night. . . . I always intended to leave.

JOHN. You never mentioned it.

TIMMY. I planned to stay a couple of weeks and then go.

JOHN. A couple of days isn't a couple of weeks.

TIMMY. It's not like I'm going to China.

JOHN. (*Crossing* R.) Why two days instead of two weeks?

TIMMY. (*Crosses* D. R.) Because I know that if I stay two weeks I'll *never* leave.

JOHN. (*Crosses above him.*) If it's what I said yesterday, about me being the boss and you'd have to do what I said—forget it.

TIMMY. It's not that. (*Crosses* L.)

JOHN. I was just letting off steam.

TIMMY. *It's not that.*

JOHN. As far as I'm concerned, you're a man— You can come and go as you please; do as you please. That goes for religion, drinking, anything.

TIMMY. How can I make you understand?

JOHN. (*Crosses to* R. *of him.*) Even girls. I know how it is to be your age. Give me a little advance notice and I'll see that you have the house to yourself whenever you want.

TIMMY. Pop, for Chris-sake.

JOHN. (*Flares momentarily.*) *What kind of language is that?* (*Then hastily; crossing* R.) I'm sorry. I didn't mean that. Talk any way you want.

TIMMY. I don't know what to say to you.

JOHN. What I said yesterday about the Jews; I was just trying to get a rise out of you.

TIMMY. I know.

JOHN. The time those bums from St. Matthew's jumped the I-cash-clothes man. I was the one who saved him.

TIMMY. I know.

JOHN. Whole crowd of people watching but I was the only one who did anything.

TIMMY. Do you think I could forget that?

JOHN. Stay another week. Just a week.

TIMMY. I can't. (*Crosses* R.)

JOHN. Stay till Wednesday.

TIMMY. (*Crosses* L.) No.

JOHN. (*Crosses to him.*) Do you have any idea how your mother looked forward to your coming home?

TIMMY. Yes.

JOHN. Then how can you do it?

TIMMY. (*Crosses* R.) We're just going around in circles.

JOHN. What happens to the lake house?

TIMMY. What do you mean?

JOHN. Without you, what's the good of it?

TIMMY. I'll be spending time there.

JOHN. I thought we'd have a real summer together like before the war.

TIMMY. (*Crosses* L.) You're making this a lot tougher than it has to be.

JOHN. (*Crosses* R. *of table.*) *Did you expect me to say nothing? Like her?*

TIMMY. Are you through?

JOHN. (*Trying a new tack; crossing to* R. *of him.*) I know what the trouble is. You know what the trouble is? You're like me. . . . Stubborn. . . . All the Clearys are stubborn. . . . Would rather die than admit a mistake. . . . Is that a fact? Yes or no?

TIMMY. I don't know.

JOHN. (*Points to himself.*) Well, here's one donkey who's seen the light. I've been wrong in my dealings with you and I admit it.

TIMMY. Pop—

JOHN. Not just wrong last night, but all along. Well, those days are gone forever, and I'll prove it. . . . You know how much money I have?

TIMMY. I don't want to know.

JOHN. Fourteen thousand three hundred and fifty-seven dollars.

TIMMY. Pop! (*Crosses* R.)

JOHN. (*Follows him.*) Plus a bit more in stocks. . . . Now *you* admit that *you* made a mistake— Admit you don't really want to leave and we'll forget the whole thing.

TIMMY. I *don't* want to leave.

JOHN. See—

TIMMY. —But I'm leaving.

JOHN. (*Turning away.*) *Then go and good riddance!* (*Crosses* D. L.)

TIMMY. Listen to me.

JOHN. The sooner the better.

TIMMY. *Listen to me!* (*Pauses—then goes on quietly, intensely.*) There was a dream I used to have about you and I. . . . It was always the same. . . . I'd be told that you were dead and I'd run crying into the street. . . . Someone would stop me and ask why I was crying and I'd say, "My father's dead and he never said he loved me."

JOHN. (*Trying unsuccessfully to shut out* TIMMY'S *words.*) I only tried to make you stay for her sake.

TIMMY. I had that dream again last night. . . . Was thinking about it this morning when something occurred to me that I'd never thought of before.

JOHN. She's the one who'll miss you.

TIMMY. It's true you've never said you love me. But it's also true that I've never said those words to you.

JOHN. I don't know what you're talking about.

TIMMY. I say them now—

JOHN. *—I don't know what you're talking about.*

TIMMY. I love you, Pop. (*He crosses to* C. JOHN'S *eyes*

squeeze shut, his entire body stiffens, as he fights to repress what he feels.) I love you.

(*For another moment,* JOHN *continues his losing battle, then, overwhelmed, turns, extends his arms.* TIMMY *goes to him. Both in tears, they embrace.* NETTIE *emerges from* TIMMY'S *room, closes the door with emphasis to alert them to her approach.* TIMMY *and* JOHN *separate hastily.*)

JOHN. (*Sotto voce.*) What I said about the money—that's strictly between us.

TIMMY. I understand.

(NETTIE *enters the kitchen. If she is aware of anything unusual in their appearance or manner, she doesn't show it.*)

NETTIE. Ready for breakfast? (*They nod; she crosses to stove for coffee pot.*) Sit down. (*They sit. She crosses to table and pours the coffee. To* TIMMY.) Your bag is packed and ready to go.

TIMMY. I've changed my mind.

NETTIE. What?

TIMMY. I've changed my mind. I'm going to stay a few more days.

JOHN. I'm afraid that's out of the question. (TIMMY *and* NETTIE *regard him incredulously.*) When you said you were going, I called the painters. They're coming in to do your room tomorrow. . . . You know how hard it is to get the painters. If we don't take them now, it'll be months before they're free again.

TIMMY. Then I guess I better leave as scheduled.

JOHN. I think so. (*To* NETTIE.) Don't you?

NETTIE. . . . Yes.

JOHN. (*He tastes the coffee—scowls.*) I don't know why I bother to bring good coffee into this house. If it isn't too weak, it's too strong. If it isn't too strong, it's too hot. If it isn't . . .

CURTAIN—THE END

PROPERTY PLOT

ACT ONE

All Props for Act One are Pre-set from Top of Show

KITCHEN:

1 beer keg D.L.
Refrigerator containing
  Prepared waffle batter in bowl with spoon
  6 bottles of beer
  Dressing
Beer opener top of refrigerator
Glasses on shelf above refrigerator
Broom closet with dressing inside
Tim's Ike jacket hanging on closet knob
Cupboards stage right
Crockery
Cups and saucers etc.
Stage left cupboards
Groceries
Sink U.C. with practical faucet
Foam rubber lining
Sink dressing
Tray lined with foam rubber
Hooks above sink 4 dish towels
Garbage pail under sink
Stove—*with*
  Coffee pot and hot coffee
  Matches—wood
  Can without label for fat
  Small fry pan aluminum
  Pot holder hanging on stove
Kitchen counter *with*
  Waffle iron D.S.
  Toaster practical with toaster cover
  Orange juice squeezer and 3 juice glasses
  Bread box with whole wheat bread (thin sliced)
  On top of bread box
    Strawberry jam
    Peach preserve
    Marmalade

3 apothecary jars with salt, rice, etc.
4 canisters (part of set including bread box) marked sugar, flour, tea, coffee
3 plates
Apron
Counter drawers
Toothpicks
Aspirin
Silverware
Counter cabinet U.S.
Vase
Kitchen table and 3 chairs
Table set for three—knife and fork on napkin, spoon on saucer
Cream and sugar bowls, creamer empty
Newspaper "Daily News" folded at John's place

Off Left:
Shopping bag with maple syrup, cream
Bag of peanuts with 5 peanuts
Roses wrapped
Brown paper bag for steak
Purse

Living Room:
Small sofa C.
Coffee table with 1946 magazines
Table U.S. sofa with candy dish
Telephone table and telephone S.R.
Armchair S.L.
Magazine rack dressed U.S. armchair and attached to it
Standing lamp U.S. armchair practical
Radio on table S.L.
Side board, dressed U.C.
John and Nettie bedroom wall dressed
Nettie's handbag—weighted and with keys

PERSONAL PROPS

TIM—Wristwatch and dogtags
JOHN—Keys, money and clip
NETTIE—Keys in bag
KITCHEN:
Table:
3 cups and saucers
Napkins

Knife on napkin
Spoon on saucer
Sugar
Cream
1 juice glass—empty

Stove:
Hot coffee
Frying pan

Refrigerator:
1 filled juice glass

Counter:
As left end act one

LIVING ROOM:
Roses—table above couch
Liquor bottle and glass in newspaper rack U.S. chair (D.L.)
Nettie's slippers under magazines on coffee table

COSTUME PLOT

ACT ONE

Scene 1:

JOHN—

Brown suit—coat, vest and trousers (1945)
Watch chain and pocket watch in vest
White shirt and brown tie
Brown socks and shoes

NETTIE—

Blue print dress—style 1945
Blue sweater on entering
Blue apron
Black pump shoes

TIMMY—

Army uniform with corporal stripes
Ribbons as described by author
Combat infantry badge

Scene 2:

John and Timmy—same as Act One, Scene 1
Nettie—Mauve dress with broach
Brown tweed coat
Brown shoes
Brown handbag

Scene 3:

Same as Act One, Scene 2

ACT TWO

Scene 1:

JOHN—

Blue suit with coat, vest, trousers
Pocket watch and chain in vest
Black socks and shoes
White shirt and blue tie

NETTIE—

Lavender dress with lace collar with broach
Black shoes

TIMMY—

Army shirt and trousers

Scene 2:
Blue suit—minus jacket
Pocket watch and chain in vest
TIMMY—as Act Two, Scene 1
NETTIE—as Act Two, Scene 1 with
Brown tweed coat
Brown gloves and bag

Scene 3:
NETTIE—
Blue bathrobe and slippers
TIMMY—
Blue plaid bathrobe
Stocking feet

Scene 4:
NETTIE—same as Act Two, Scene 3
JOHN—
Brown suit of Act One (no jacket)
TIMMY—
Army shirt and trousers

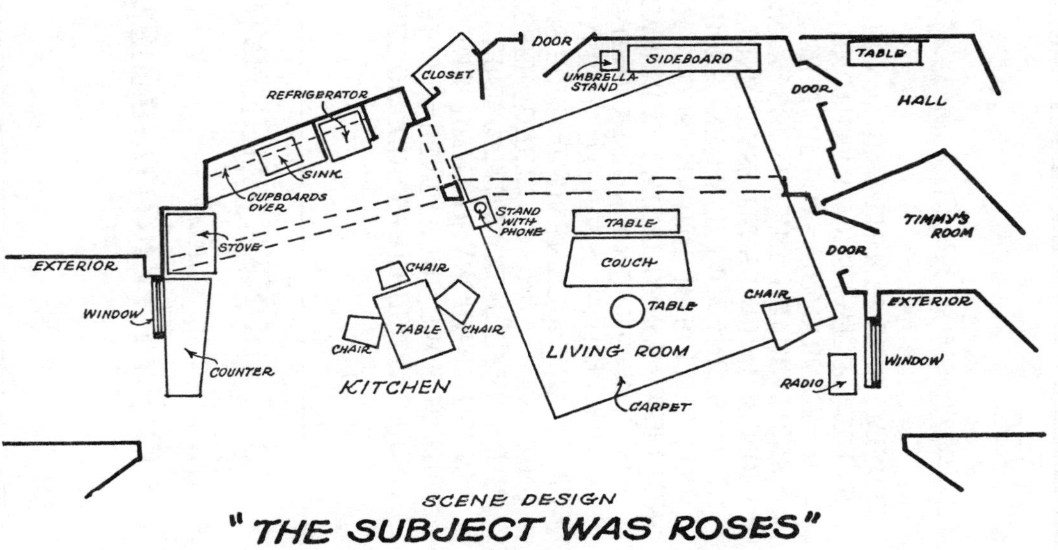

SCENE DESIGN

"THE SUBJECT WAS ROSES"

Other Publications for Your Interes

SEA MARKS

(LITTLE THEATRE—DRAMA)

By GARDNER McKAY

1 woman, 1 man—Unit set

Winner of L.A. Drama Critics Circle Award "Best Play." This is the "funny, touching, bittersweet tale" (Sharbutt, A.P.) of a fisherman living on a remote island to the west of Ireland who has fallen in love with, in retrospect, a woman he's glimpsed only once. Unschooled in letter-writing, he tries his utmost to court by mail and, after a year-and-a-half, succeeds in arranging a rendezvous at which, to his surprise, she persuades him to live with her in Liverpool. Their love affair ends only when he is forced to return to the life he better understands. "A masterpiece." (The Tribune, Worcester, Mass.) "Utterly winning," (John Simon, New York Magazine.) "There's abundant humor, surprisingly honest humor, that grows between two impossible partners. The reaching out and the fearful withdrawal of two people who love each other but whose lives simply cannot be fused: a stubborn, decent, attractive and touching collision of temperments, honest in portraiture and direct in speech. High marks for SEA MARKS!" (Walter Kerr, New York Times.) "Fresh as a May morning. A lovely, tender and happily humorous love story." (Elliot Norton, Boston Herald American.) "It could easily last forever in actors' classrooms and audition studios." (Oliver, The New Yorker)

THE WOOLGATHERER

(LITTLE THEATRE—DRAMA)

By WILLIAM MASTROSIMONE

1 man, 1 woman—Interior

In a dreary Philadelphia apartment lives Rose, a shy and slightly creepy five-and-dime salesgirl. Into her life saunters Cliff, a hard-working, hard-drinking truck driver—who has picked up Rose and been invited back to her room. Rose is an innocent whose whole life centers around reveries and daydreams. He is rough and witty—but it's soon apparent—just as starved for love as she is. This little gem of a play was a recent success at New York's famed Circle Repertory starring Peter Weller and Patricia Wettig. Actors take note: *The Woolgatherer* has several excellent monologues. ". . . energy, compassion and theatrical sense are there."—N.Y. Times. ". . . another emotionally wrenching experience no theatre enthusiast should miss."—Rex Reed. "Mastrosimone writes consistently witty and sometimes lyrical dialogue."—New York Magazine. "(Mastrosimone) has a knack for composing wildly humorous lines at the same time that he is able to penetrate people's hearts and dreams."—Hollywood Reporter.

...eeze from The Gulf

MART CROWLEY

(Little Theatre) Drama

... "The Boys in the Band" takes us on a journey ... all Mississippi town to watch a 15-year-old boy su... ...gh adolescence to adulthood and success as a writer. His mother is a frilly southern doll who has nothing to fall back on when her beauty fades. She develops headaches and other physical problems, while the asthmatic son turns to dolls and toys at an age when other boys are turning to sports. The traveling father becomes withdrawn, takes to drink; and mother takes to drugs to kill the pain of the remembrances of things past. She eventually ends in an asylum, and the father in his fumbling way tries to tell the son to live the life he must.

"The boy is plunged into a world of suffering he didn't create. . . . One of the most electrifying plays I've seen in the past few years . . . Scenes boil and hiss . . . The dialogue goes straight to the heart." Reed, Sunday News.

ECHOES

N. RICHARD NASH

(All Groups) Drama

2 Men, 1 Woman, Interior

A young man and woman build a low-keyed paradise of happiness within an asylum, only to have it shattered by the intrusion of the outside world. The two characters search, at times agonizingly to determine the difference between illusion and reality. The effort is lightened at times by moments of shared love and "pretend" games, like decorating Christmas trees that are not really there. The theme of love, vulnerable to the surveillances of the asylum, and the ministrations of the psychiatrist, (a non-speaking part) seems as fragile in the constrained setting as it often is in the outside world.

". . . even with the tragic, sombre theme there is a note of hope and possible release and the situations presented specifically also have universal applications to give it strong effect . . . intellectual, but charged with emotion."—Reed.